AMERICAN HOOKED AND SEWN RUGS

AMERICAN HOOKED AND SEWN RUGS

FOLK ART UNDERFOOT

Joel and Kate Kopp

NEW YORK
E. P. DUTTON & CO., INC.
1975

Color plate, page 1: Twentieth-century images find their way into the repertory of hooked rug designs. Just as earlier rugmakers had chosen to portray subjects close to their hearts, such as their horses, so the maker of this rug must have been quite proud of the family car and has included the details of the radiator grille, the subtle nuance of glossy window glass, and even the make of this once-well-known automobile. c. 1920. 26″ x 34″.

Color plate, page 2: The vividness of the freely drawn stripes and dots gives this piece the exuberance of a field of flags: 1920–1930. 72″ x 39″.

Illustration, above: Hattie Klapp Brunner is a lady in her eighties who paints watercolors based on her memories of life in Pennsylvania as it was when she was growing up. On the front porch in her painting a girl is cutting the fabric strips to be used in the rooster rug the woman is hooking in the yard. The cat has been included, Hattie told us, because he always came running to play with the dangling strips. Watercolor. 1975. 6½″ x 8½″.

Color plate, page 5: Vivid colors in two chevron bands emphasize the warmth of this welcome mat. c. 1895. 22½″ x 39″.

Color plate, page 6: The flame-stitch pattern, long popular in embroidery, is effectively used in this stairway runner. c. 1885. 138″ x 18½″.

Designed by Joel and Kate Kopp.

CONTENTS

ACKNOWLEDGMENTS

Kay Hines and Susan Wallblom Malone worked closely with us in researching and assembling this book, and both deserve special thanks and recognition. Other friends who gave us their time and their ideas were Jack Ericson, Davida Deutsch, Ed Clein, Barbara Traub, and Gene Traub. They and the following individuals were especially helpful and enthusiastic, and we thank all of them.

Max Allen; Shiela Betterton; Robert Bishop; Henry Coger; Quintina Colio; Priscilla Creamer; Judith Dawes; Irene Dodge; Gisele Folsam; Richard C. Frantz; Dieter Froese; Leslie Geddes-Brown; Barry Greenlaw; Bruce Johnson; Marilyn Bordes Johnson; C. R. Jones; Arthur Leibundguth; Judy Lenett; Nina Fletcher Little; Bates Lowry; Larry Majeski; Florence Maine; Edward E. Nickels; Eleanor Nowlin; Jane C. Nylander; Virginia Parslow Partridge; Sam Pennington; Betty Ring; Sidney and Phyllis Rosner; Walter Simmons II; R. Scudder Smith; Diane Solomon; Susan Swann; Elizabeth Tobin; Simon Waegemaekers.

Grateful acknowledgment is also made to the following individuals, institutions, shops, and galleries for providing the material reproduced here.

Antiquarian and Landmarks Society, Inc., of Connecticut, Hartford, Connecticut; Mr. and Mrs. David Bakalar; The Barenholtz Collection; George and Janet Bookman; Mr. and Mrs. Edwin Braman; Brown-Trump Farm, Medina, Ohio; Bury Farm Antiques, Morrisville, New York; Ed Clein Antiques, New York; Country Inn Antiques, York Springs, Pennsylvania; James Crawford; The Cunninghams, Denver, Pennsylvania; Allan L. Daniel, New York; Davida Deutsch Antiques, New York; Michael and Mary Erlanger; Burton and Helaine Fendelman, Scarsdale, New York; Mary Mac Franklin; Jane Gair; Hovey Gleason Antiques, Marietta, Pennsylvania; Mr. and Mrs. Peter Goodman; Greenfield Village and Henry Ford Museum, Dearborn, Michigan; Richard and Nelle Hankinson; Hart-Tapley Antiques, Lynnfield Center, Massachusetts; Hastings House Antiques, Essex, Connecticut; Herbert W. Hemphill, Jr.; The Henry Francis du Pont Winterthur Museum, Winterthur, Delaware; Hidden River Antiques, Scarsdale, New York; Timothy and Pamela Hill, South Lyon, Michigan; Hirschl & Adler Galleries, Inc., New York; Jonathan Holstein and Gail van der Hoof; Eliot Hubbard; Dahlov Ipcar; Carroll and Wendy Janis; Barbara Johnson; Douglas Leroy Joslin, New York; Steven and Helen Kellogg; Kelter-Malcé Antiques, New York; Ron and Anita Klink; Monique Knowlton; Ronald and Marilyn Kowaleski, Wernersville, Pennsylvania; James Kronen Gallery, New York; Judy and Paul Lenett; Bertram K. and Nina Fletcher·Little; Sanford and Balene McCormick; Sara Melvin; The Metropolitan Museum of Art, New York; Mr. and Mrs. Ben Mildwoof; The Naga Shop, New York; The Newark Museum, Newark, New Jersey; New Hampshire Historical Society, Concord, New Hampshire; New York State Historical Association, Cooperstown, New York; Old Glory Antiques, Woodstock, New York; Old Sturbridge Village, Sturbridge, Massachusetts; Pine Cone Antiques, New York; Burt Purmell, New York; Putnam and Smith, Ipswich, Massachusetts; George E. Schoellkopf Gallery, New York; Kathy Schoemer Antiques, New Canaan, Connecticut; Shakertown at Pleasant Hill, Kentucky, Inc., Harrodsburg, Kentucky; The Shelburne Museum, Shelburne, Vermont; Beatrice Shilstone; John and Jacqueline Sideli, Malden Bridge, New York; Silver Spring Farm, Ridgefield, Connecticut; Mr. and Mrs. Walter Simmons; Smithsonian Institution, Washington, D.C.; Sotheby Parke Bernet Inc., New York; Nina Howell Starr; Penelope Comfort Starr; Gary and Nancy Stass; Betty Sterling, Randolph, Vermont; Dalmar A. Tifft; Barbara Traub; Mr. and Mrs. Harley N. Trice II; Donald and Faye Walters; Wenham Historical Association and Museum, Inc., Wenham, Massachusetts; Joseph and Ellen Wetherell, Bedford Hills, New York; and lastly, a very special thank you to Cyril I. Nelson, our editor, who helped us every step along the way.

Notes on the plates: Height precedes width. All hooked rugs have a burlap foundation unless otherwise indicated. Rugs to which no ownership has been ascribed are in the authors' collection or have been provided by America Hurrah Antiques, New York City.

INTRODUCTION

It is our intent to bring a new eye to hooked and sewn rugs. The primitive imagery that appears in these rugs often parallels the more accepted forms of folk art, but rugs have rarely received the same recognition. As with much of functional American folk art, these rugs have been neglected, ill-treated, and inadequately appreciated for decades. This may be because most were not made to be "art" but to serve as floor coverings for the parlor or bedroom, or even as kitchen or hall mats. They were a practical solution to a household need, yet the rugs brought color, warmth, and decoration to sometimes primitive and lonely environments. Rugmaking gave country women (who might never have given their time to painting) a way to create pictures and geometric designs. Generally without academic art training, many rugmakers could intuitively sense the power of form and color, and their pictorial or graphic statements were not inhibited by the difficulties involved in translating perspective and fine detail into rugs. These pieces frequently exhibit masterful needlework, but their primary appeal to us is as visual statements and not as needlecraft.

The choice of illustrations does not reflect an effort to show the most typical examples. Rather, we are presenting here a chronological visual record of American rugs that we consider to be folk art. For the most part we have excluded the great body of uninspired rugs that were made from commercially manufactured patterns. Patterns made rugmaking easier and helped popularize the craft after the Civil War. But by eliminating the need to design, they stifled originality and creativity among those introduced to hooking through these precut and stenciled burlap rug bases. Fortunately, many great, original, and individualistic rugs were still made after patterns became available.

Rugmaking was essentially a simple craft, and its flexibility encouraged a wide range of designs, but artistry was often sublimated to practicality. Most of the hooked rugs we have seen lack originality and spirit and can best be put into the category of "decoration." Only a very small percentage of the rugs have that primitive force and unique naïve character that transform them into folk art. A hooked rug with crude drawing or poor perspective is not necessarily a piece of folk art. We believe that to constitute true folk art, the design must not only have a strong sense of space and color, but also a feeling of feedback from the emotions and sensibilities of the maker. The makers put something of themselves into these rugs through their intuitive artistry, and even the rags that were hooked into them were very often their own family clothing remnants, each with a personal history.

Although the emphasis of this book is visual and not historical, we shall be tracing the origins and development of hooked and sewn rugs in America from their beginnings in eighteenth-century New England bed rugs to twentieth-century examples. In explaining when, where, and how these rugs were made and in briefly describing the methods and materials used, we hope to help collectors to determine the age, category, and relative rarity of rugs they have found. A great deal of misinformation has been disseminated about hooked and sewn rugs over the years, and we hope to clarify some confusing points. However, this is not a "how to" book for those interested in making a rug. Much of the specific technical information will be found in the footnotes and in the captions that accompany the illustrations. We have also included advice for the care, cleaning, and storage of hooked and sewn rugs (see page 125).

Hooked and sewn rugs represent an important segment of American design. The best are outstanding examples of American folk art and represent a tradition of giving everyday household objects a decorative individuality and beauty that exemplifies what Millet called "A treating of the commonplace with a feeling of the sublime."

JOEL AND KATE KOPP

BED RUGS

Prior to 1800 the floors in most American homes were kept bare. The American textile industry was still in its infancy, and it was not until about 1830 that significant amounts of finished yard goods and carpeting were produced domestically. Manufactured goods were imported at great expense, making it necessary for most Americans to make cloth at home from native raw materials. The processes of converting raw wool or flax into cloth were complex and arduous. Textiles were needed for necessities such as clothing, bedding, and linens, and even when used decoratively, textiles were far too valuable to be trampled underfoot. Ingrain and machine-loomed Wilton or Brussels carpets imported from Europe could be bought only by the wealthiest American families, and even in these prosperous homes their use was reserved for the best rooms. Handmade Oriental carpets and the European "Turkey Work" imitations were rarely used on the floor during the first half of the eighteenth century. These household treasures were displayed on tables and chests and are often prominently featured in portraits of the period. It was not uncommon for sand to be used to cover kitchen and parlor floors. The sand was spread evenly over the floor and then brushed with a broom into swirls, scrolls, and herringbone designs. The sand held and absorbed grease and dirt, and the geometric effects were pleasing if not long lasting. Sand decoration was probably the only floor covering that was used in the eighteenth century by rich and poor alike. Even the woven straw mats and painted canvas floorcloths popular then were usually imported and available only to the affluent.

Until about 1820 *rugg* meant a coarse woolen cloth or bedcover. Most of the "ruggs" made by Americans in the eighteenth and the first decade of the nineteenth century covered their beds and furniture and not their floors.

The bed (with its furnishings) was the most valuable piece of furniture in Colonial homes, and its decoration was usually the single most important piece of needlework that a woman of the period would attempt. Whether it was a quilted linsey-woolsey coverlet, a pieced or appliquéd patchwork quilt, a crewel counterpane or a sewn bed rug, the making of the bedcover was an opportunity for artistic creation and was often the tour de force of a woman's sewing skills.

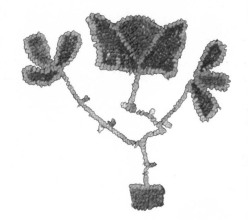

1 (above), 1a (opposite). This second-earliest-known bed rug was made in 1724 in Ipswich, Massachusetts, by Catherine Thorn for the wedding chest of her sister Mary. The purity of the design and the use of bold animal silhouettes are virtually unique among bed rugs. The strength of the simple forms in this piece remarkably anticipates some of the outstanding hooked rugs produced over a century and a half later. Running stitch with clipped pile on linsey-woolsey. Dated 1724; initialed C.T. 91″ x 84″. (Wenham Historical Association and Museum, Inc.)

Bed rugs were almost always made on a woolen base with thick multi-plied, home-dyed, woolen yarns sewn through with a running stitch to create the design. Most of the surviving bed rugs were made in Connecticut, and virtually all were made in New England. They frequently had exotic floral motifs in the manner of English and East Indian textiles, or wallpaper and embroidery patterns, but many display an individuality that makes bed rugs an important and uniquely American form of needlework. Bed rugs made in England appear in seventeenth- and eighteenth-century inventories, and although no examples of these English bed rugs have survived, we know that they were simple and undecorated woolens, sometimes woven in stripes and plaids.

The bed rug has a long history in Scandinavia, where even in fifteenth-century Finland *ryijys* were used to cover beds and as tapestries to cover walls on festive occasions.[1] The Finnish rugs were made in the manner of Oriental carpets; that is, the loops of wool used to form the decoration were tied as the base was being woven on the loom. It appears that the use of the simple running stitch that formed loops (which were sometimes clipped) on the woven foundation of a bed rug is an American decorative innovation. Bed rugs, after years of use, have in rare cases been known to be used as floor coverings, but it should be noted that bed rugs are *not* hooked rugs, although they have frequently been mislabeled as such.

The bed rugs we have illustrated are similar in design to floor rugs made later. Catherine Thorn's rug (fig. 1), made in 1724, is dramatic and primitive and remarkably anticipates the style of later hooked rugs. Most bed rugs have an overall design that covers virtually the entire surface of the rug. The animal forms silhouetted against the solid background of this bed rug and its open spaciousness are most unusual in bed rugs.

The creation of a bed rug must have been a proud and important event, since most bear the initials of the maker and the year in which the rug was made. Mary Comstock might be called the "John Hancock" of bed-rug makers. Her name and "Jany 30, 1810" boldly fill the upper quarter of her rug (fig. 2). (Names, epigrams, and even poems were frequently worked into *hooked*

2 (left). Mary Comstock was 66 years old when she made this rug in Shelburne, Vermont. The design is simple, bold, and direct, and we conjecture that these were qualities that Mary Comstock possessed herself. She died in 1828 at the age of 84, and her signed rug passed through many owners, traveling as far as Minnesota, until it finally came back to Shelburne in 1956. Running stitch on homespun plaid wool. Brown background with flowers in blues, tans, and brown. Dated January 30, 1810. 87″ x 78″. (Shelburne Museum, Inc.)

rugs, especially at the end of the nineteenth and during the early twentieth century.)

Very few bed rugs have survived (the number may be fewer than fifty), and prior to the important exhibition of bed rugs held at the Wadsworth Atheneum in Hartford, Connecticut, in 1972 very little was really known about these rare American bedcoverings. The show, "Bed Ruggs/1722–1833," was assembled by J. Herbert Callister and included thirty-four examples. Even those who missed seeing the exhibit can appreciate the tapestrylike effect these rugs had when they were hung, for all were illustrated in the catalogue written by William L. Warren—the most informative work on the subject available. Our readers are also referred to the chapter "The Bed Rug" in *America's Quilts and Coverlets* by Carleton L. Safford and Robert Bishop and the articles in The Magazine *Antiques* that have appeared over the last fifty years.

Great effort was required to make a bed rug, both in the creation of large quantities of hand-spun and home-dyed materials and in the designing and sewing of the rug itself. The results of these efforts gave a Colonial bedroom warmth and elegance. In the eighteenth century the pleasures of bed rugs were frequently shared with the ubiquitous bedbug that sometimes was "snug as a bug in a rug."[2]

3 (opposite, above), 3a (right). This casual design is a pleasant contrast to the balanced formality seen in most bed rugs. The geometric sunflower acts as a strong center for the surrounding sprawl of meandering buds, vines, and blossoms. The use of flower and leaf patterns to form a broad border is a device much used in later hooked rugs. Running stitch with clipped pile wool. c. 1820. 90″ x 83″. (Antiquarian and Landmarks Society, Inc., of Connecticut)

4 (opposite, below), 4a (opposite, below right). This unusual geometric bed rug utilizes the "clamshell" motif in a dramatic contrast of lights and darks. Running stitch on wool. Indigo blues, white, and dark brown. Dated 1783; initialed RWB. 90″ x 87″. (The Henry Francis du Pont Winterthur Museum)

YARN-SEWN RUGS

By the end of the eighteenth century Oriental rugs and "Turkey carpets" were being used on the floor. Imported rugs and manufactured carpets became more common in households, but the custom of covering tables and chests with rugs persisted, and many yarn-sewn rugs made during the first quarter of the nineteenth century were designed for this purpose. Some yarn-sewn rugs may have been made in wealthier homes to protect the imported carpet near the hearth from sparks, ashes, and soot. It must again be noted that American carpet mills did not begin production until about 1825, and since imported carpet was extremely valuable, the precaution of making a rug to protect it was considered prudent and fashionable. The most extensive use of yarn-sewn rugs was as a cover for the hearthstone during the summer months. (The *Oxford English Dictionary* of 1810 makes note of "a little rug for your hearthstone."[3])

The use of hearthrugs seems to have begun in America around 1800. An advertisement in the *New York Gazette and General Advertiser* of May 22, 1799, offered for sale "An assortment of hearth rugs."[4] Ten years later, Jefferson's inventory of the presidential mansion included "1 elegant Brussels carpet and a fire rug."[5] Noah Webster defined a *rug* as "a woolen cloth used for a bedcover, and in modern times [1828], particularly for covering the carpet before the fireplace."[6] The use of a rug on the hearth in summer is illustrated in H. Knight's painting, *The Family at Home* (fig. 5).

The earliest dated yarn-sewn rug we know of was made in 1824 (fig. 14). Unfortunately, unlike bed rugs, yarn-sewn rugs are rarely dated, although we do know that the majority were made between 1800 and 1840.[7] Yarn-sewn rugs were usually made with two-ply yarn on a base of homespun linen or on a grain bag. Worked with nautical motifs on a canvas base, the rug in figure 9 suggests that some of these yarn-sewn rugs were designed and possibly even executed by sailors during their long voyages. The yarn was sewn through the base fabric with a continuous running stitch, leaving loops on the surface that formed and followed the shape of the design. Usually the loops were clipped leaving a soft pile as a surface. Sometimes a reed, a quill, or a similar

5 (above). Detail from *The Family at Home*, painted by H. Knight in 1836. In this glimpse into the parlor of a prosperous Connecticut family, a sewn rug is seen covering the hearthstone, with summer decorations filling the fireplace. The entire scene is repeated in the painting within the painting that hangs above the mantel. Oil on canvas. 26¾" x 35⅝". (Hirschl & Adler Galleries, Inc.)

6 (above), 6a (right). An unrestrained imagination and a strong artistic intuition are expressed in this rug. Mammoth flowers reach out over houses no bigger than toys and strong geometric forms are randomly placed, creating a powerful and eccentric composition. The artist's unconventional vision transforms this rug into a fantasy garden of magical impossibilities. Yarn-sewn on madder-dyed linen, c. 1800. 17¼" x 29¼". (Jonathan Holstein and Gail van der Hoof)

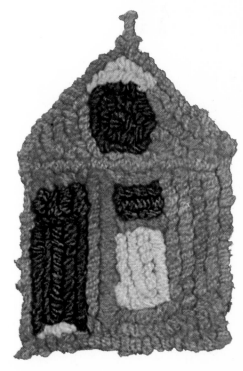

15

7 (above), 7a (below). Ohio became the seventeenth state to enter the Union in 1803, followed by Louisiana in 1812. The American eagle with its shield, arrows, and olive branches is mantled by seventeen stars, and this rug would appear to have been made within this nine-year period. Initialed "P A L." Found in Oneida, New York. Yarn-sewn on linen. Madder red, blues, and creams. 36″ x 69″. (Constance Noyes Robertson; photograph courtesy New York State Historical Association)

flexible device was used to regulate the height of the loops of the pile, which explains why yarn-sewn rugs have sometimes been referred to as *reed-stitched*.[8]

These yarn-sewn rugs should not be confused with later *hooked* rugs in which yarn is used. The great majority of hooked rugs are made on burlap, whereas yarn-sewn rugs, with rare exceptions, were sewn on linen. A surer way to distinguish the two types is by looking at the undersurface of the rug. The back of a yarn-sewn rug has a dotted appearance with most of the surface of the linen base showing (see fig. 9a). The back of a hooked rug repeats the design of the front with little or none of the burlap showing. (Illustrations of both techniques and of the backs of the rugs are on pages 122–123.)

After the Revolution an "American spirit" developed, and its influence was felt in all forms of creative ex-

8 (above), 8a (below). The name "J. M. Talpey," partially obscured by wear, is sewn into the lower portion of this rug. The packet ship *John Talpey* (named for the famous navy captain who fought in the War of 1812) flies the Black Ball Line pennant and is pictured sailing from what is probably New York harbor with the fort on Governors Island at the left. Yarn-sewn on canvas. Azure blue, olive green, and mauve. c. 1825. 60″ x 32″. (Formerly in the C. M. Traver Collection; photograph reproduced from auction catalogue of American Art Galleries, New York, April 18, 1925)

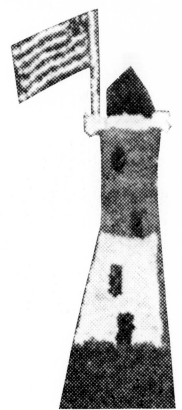

pression. Patriotic motifs became prevalent after the War of 1812 and reliance on English design traditions abated. Samplers, quilts, and yarn-sewn rugs reflected this trend toward more originality in design. People, houses, ships, and animals, as well as dramatic geometric forms, replaced the balanced floral and tilelike geometric designs that were prevalent in the seventeenth and eighteenth centuries. The makers of yarn-sewn rugs and other forms of needlework began to use their imaginations. Fantasy and bold use of space characterized many of their designs, and the proportions of the elements in each rug were determined by their own artistic needs.

Yarn-sewn rugs are rare, and even worn examples should be treasured. They are the first, and we believe the most beautiful, form of pictorial American floor rugs, and they established a tradition of rugmaking that has lasted into the twentieth century.

9 (above). Although we cannot be certain that this rug was actually made by a sailor, there is persuasive evidence that seamen's handicrafts contributed significantly to the art of rugmaking. Obviously of nautical inspiration, this yarn-sewn rug is worked on canvas, and the foreign flags in three of the corners presumably represent ports of call. The way in which the forms are composed and balanced is methodically planned out. Even the shape of the anchor is subtly echoed in an extraordinary stylized eagle with its curious ropelike neck. The sweeping V of the eagle's wings and the stripes of its emblematic body are beautifully consistent with the flags and banded diamond shapes. A detail of the reverse of the American flag showing the yarn-sewn technique is illustrated on the opposite page. c. 1810. 26″ x 52″. (The Smithsonian Institution, Hall of American Maritime Enterprise; gift of Tessin Zorach)

9a (opposite, below). Enlarged detail of the reverse side of the American flag in rug above showing yarn sewn through the canvas foundation.

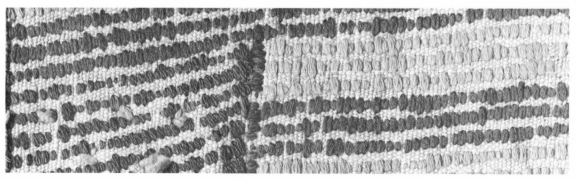

11 (above). A traditional basket of flowers sitting on a fragile candlestand looms
improbably large in a landscape where tiny lambs make their way like unsteady ants.
The innocence of the crude draftsmanship and the combination of unlikely motifs have
the charm and appeal of the true naïve imagination. Found in southern New Hampshire.
Yarn-sewn on cotton. Blue, gray, green, tan, and brown. c. 1810. 58″ x 24″.
(Betty Sterling)

12 (above). Stool covers were frequently made from remnants of damaged or worn yarn-sewn rugs. This example, however, with its graphic radial flower, appears to have been made specifically for the stool it covers. Yarn-sewn on linen. c. 1820. 8″ x 11″. (William C. Putnam and Beverly T. Smith)

10 (left). This large yarn-sewn rug looks as if it could be a design for a sampler done by a schoolgirl at a young ladies' academy during the early part of the nineteenth century. The making of a sampler was almost always a basic part of the curriculum, but rugmaking is only very rarely mentioned in advertisements for these schools. In Boston, a Mrs. Davis, advertising her "Boarding and Day School" in *The Columbian Centinel* of March 21, 1810. offered in addition to ". . . patterns of the most fashionable and elegant needlework of all kinds," instruction in ". . . tambour, embroidery, rugs and other worsted work, . . ." Yarn-sewn on linen. c. 1825. 36″ x 69½″. (New York State Historical Association)

13 (above). In this landscape the trees have been handled in a fairly naturalistic yet highly expressive manner. Somewhat oversized squirrels perch in the bare branches of on tree, while flattened shapes of sheep and cows roam the meadow in the foreground. c. 1825. 22″ x 50″.

14 (above). This impressive rug, initialed "P. S." by the maker and dated 1824, is the earliest dated yarn-sewn rug we know of. Birds and flowers and two lambs stand out from the dark background. 24″ x 76″. (Private collection)

15 (opposite, below). A rare combination of yarn sewing with shirring used as an inner border. (Shirring is discussed on page 28.) A house of madder-red wool is set solidly within a flux of windblown blues. Even with this restricted color range, the maker has conveyed the feeling of a home, the center of warmth and stability,

withstanding the turbulent elements. Wool, yarn-sewn and chenille-shirred, on linen. c. 1830. 46″ x 60″.

16 (below). The formal symmetry of the decorated urns with their overflowing bouquets suggests the elegance of very genteel surroundings. Technically, the rug is an exceptional example of yarn sewing, with its thick rich pile and closely sewn stitches. Found in Massachusetts. Yarn-sewn on linen. First quarter of the nineteenth century. 33″ x 63″. (George E. Schoellkopf Gallery)

17 (above), 17a (opposite, above). These appealing lions stare quizzically out of their Eden-like setting. The rug has the same biblical quality that some of Edward Hicks's *Peaceable Kingdom* paintings convey. Bordered on three sides by strong geometrics, the ground of this semitropical landscape acts to complete the frame. Yarn-sewn on linen with fringed border. c. 1810. 50½" x 24". (Old Sturbridge Village)

18 (opposite, below), 19 (above). Both of these rugs were found in southern Maine and were very probably made by the same person. The interplay of colors results in startling positive-negative reverberations. This kind of pure geometry is extremely rare in early rugmaking, but it is frequently seen in decorated furniture and boxes made in Maine at that time. Although the rugs are of a very early period, their designs are in some ways strikingly modern in feeling. Yarn-sewn on linen. Both first quarter of the nineteenth century. Fig. 18: 82″ x 34½″; fig. 19: 76″ x 32½″. (Private collection)

20 (above). *The Tiger*, a woodcut illustration in Thomas Bewick's *The Quadrupeds*, published in Philadelphia in 1810, is believed to be the inspiration for this whiskered Bengal. Wild-animal shows are known to have existed in America even in 1820, but most rugmakers had to rely on woodcuts or engravings as models for their exotic animal subjects. Yarn-sewn on linen. White, rust, brown, and green. c. 1820. 41¼" x 67". (The Shelburne Museum, Inc.)

21 (above), 21a (opposite, below). This unusual rug shows us the virtues and vices of the citizens of a Massachusetts town. A truant schoolboy flinches under rod of his schoolmaster, while to their right, a pious matron enters the front door of the church, apparently disregarding a local gunner taking potshots at birds on the church roof. Enigmatic letters, perhaps sets of initials, are randomly placed throughout the rug. Found in southeastern Massachusetts. Yarn-sewn on linen. Dated 1828. 32" x 72". (Private collection)

22 (above). In this wonderfully sentimental rug touching hearts are placed within an oval garland and set inside a bountiful diamond-shaped garden. Equally bountiful cats and their kittens stare out quizzically. Yarn-sewn on linen. First quarter of the nineteenth century. 24″ x 50″ (Paul and Judy Lenett)

SHIRRED RUGS

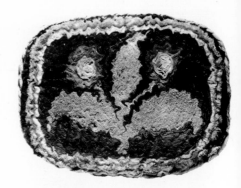

At the beginning of the nineteenth century fabric mills sprang up all over New England. Although inexpensive printed cotton goods soon became readily available, creative women still saved scraps of fabric and old clothing, frequently utilizing them for quiltmaking. After 1830 American mills began large-scale production of machine-made carpeting. The availability of the more modestly priced American-made carpeting soon created a vogue for covered floors. Women even began to look to their scrap bags for new ways to create homemade rugs. It is during this period that braided rugs first appear. (We illustrate a remarkable example of a braided rug in figure 35.) The technique of *shirring* also seems to have started around this same time. Shirring is an appliqué technique that was developed because cloth strips were far thicker than yarn and could not be *sewn through* a woven linen or cotton fabric base.

The most popular technique used in making shirred rugs was the *chenille* method. Strips of cloth one-half inch to one and one-half inches wide were sewn down the center with a running stitch. The cloth was then gathered into folds by pulling the thread, after which the gathered cloth strip resembled a fabric caterpillar. These "caterpillars" were then stitched to a base of linen, cotton, or even a rough grain bag. In a shirred rug the fabric lies on the top surface, and only the thread stitches show on the back of the rug.

The second method of shirring used fabric that was cut on the bias into strips about one inch wide. These strips were then folded in half and the folded edge was sewn to the surface, following and forming the intended design. The folded strips were sewn closely side by side so that one strip held up the next, and the raw edges formed the pile (figs. 23, 23a). A variant of this technique appears in figures 28 and 28a. This rug is made with an interesting and rarely used method of shirring that we call *pleated shirring*. This technique is described and illustrated on page 31. Diagrams of the chenille, bias, and pleated shirring techniques appear on pages 122–123.

23, 23a (above). Bias shirring was extremely rare in any form due to the exacting nature of the technique. Here it is used in a simple composition of two flowers, bordered to fit the shape of the small stool for which it was intended. Appliquéd to a home-woven base with a cotton herringbone warp over a horsehair weft. Braided woolen border. c. 1830. 10″ x 11½″.

24 (right). Full bunches of grapes balance the curling floral forms in this shirred rug. An image of abundance against an almost tropical orange ground. Quick black strokes add an effective and unusual border. Wool, chenille-shirred on cotton ticking. 1850–1860. 21¼″ x 58½″. (Betty Sterling)

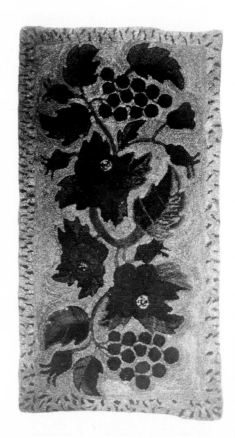

25 (above). This happy house is framed by two apple trees that would be a botanist's delight. The two white stripes help support and define the house set against a dark two-color ground that is punctuated by bright flowers. Chenille-shirred on linen. c. 1850. 34″ x 58¾″. (Private collection)

26 (above). The sturdy shapes in this rug have the innocence and confidence of a child's drawing. The technique, however, is quite sophisticated, with tightly shirred woolens creating a full rich surface texture. The shirred caterpillars of the background set up a subtle rippling effect that echoes the forms of the flowers. Chenille-shirred on linen. 1830–1850. 34″ x 63″. (Stephen and Helen Kellogg)

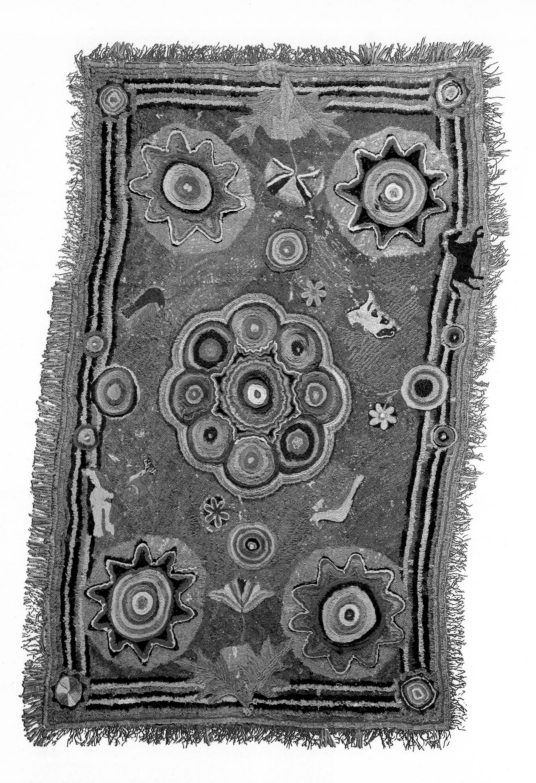

27 (above). The daring to experiment both in conception and technique has produced this extraordinary rug that combines shirring with wool stitching. The maker had apparently become captivated by the new technique of bias shirring. Explosive shirred stars set around a cluster of shirred spirals dominate the composition. Wonderful embroidered animals are strewn freely over a celestial blue, and the maker has even allowed her menagerie to wander beyond the limits of the border. This totally unorthodox breaking of the border is an adventure in design we have not seen in any rugs made before or since. Bias shirring, yarn sewing, and embroidery stitching on linen with a fringed border. c. 1825. 35½" x 55¼". (The Henry Francis du Pont Winterthur Museum)

28 (right), 28a (below). This rug employs a rarely used shirring technique—*pleated shirring*. With this technique the maker has created a complex grid of dark hues of subtle variation. The brilliance of the most inventive rugmakers lies in their ability to use design elements that are similar but never exactly the same to achieve the impression of symmetry without repetition. In this rug strips of tightly woven woolens were stitched widthwise to the base, then looped up and stitched down again, fold after fold, with each fold set tightly against the preceding one, until a rectangular section of dense intricate ribboning was produced. Sections of varied widths and lengths comprise a field of folds cut through by curving vines made of the same pleated shirring. (A diagram of pleated shirring appears on page 122.) The red blossoms are chenille-shirred. Base and surface of woven woolens. 1830–1850. 40¾″ x 87½″. (Private collection)

Shirred rugs were also made with lengths of knitted yarn (usually one to four inches wide), which were folded and the edges were sewn down to the base, leaving the fold upright. The folds were sewn closely together, and when the rug was completed, the folds were cut open with a scissors. The knit would ravel with use, developing a soft furry surface. The rug illustrated in figure 62 is an unusual example combining hooking and ravel-pile shirring. This ravel-pile technique appears to have been popular in Vermont, New Hampshire, and Maine from about 1880 to 1910.

In another shirring technique, sometimes called *patch shirring*, small circular or square pieces of fabric were folded or bunched and then sewn at the apex to the base fabric. We have also seen a rug that has small bundles of yarn sewn with thread on a linen base, forming a floral design. Rugs of this type were also made in Scotland.

We know of no dated examples of shirred rugs, but most of the ones we have examined appear to have been made between 1825 and 1860. The decline in the shirring technique seems to correspond to the rising popularity, at the end of the 1850s, of rugs hooked on burlap. Both hooked and shirred rugs utilized cloth scraps, but hooked rugs proved to be more durable and easier to make. They also allowed a greater flexibility in delineating forms and figures. Shirred rugs made before the Civil War are very rare and are highly prized by collectors.

29 (above). This is one of several shirred rugs made in Maine by a Mrs. Sawyer during the 1880s and 1890s. Geometric patterns are not commonly found in shirred rugs but this relatively late example of the technique reflects an awareness of a popular hooked rug design, suggesting basket weave. c. 1890. 30″ x 45″.

30 (below). The difficulty of rendering pictorial images with bias shirring accounts for the rarity of examples. This piece uses the technique successfully, creating the distinctive fluted vibrations characteristic of bias shirring. Second quarter of the nineteenth century. 27½″ x 55″. (Formerly in the C. M. Traver Collection; photograph reproduced from auction catalogue of the American Art Galleries, New York, April 18, 1925.)

31 (above). The border and central elements in this rug are caterpillar-shirred with large areas of yarn sewing in the blue sky and brown midground. Bright red accents in the chimneys and the plumage of the birds in the tree between the houses stand out from the overall soft brown tones of the piece. c. 1835. 27″ x 52″. (Private collection)

32 (below). William Henry Harrison on horseback and the log cabin he made famous as an emblem of his presidential campaign in the election of 1840 are yarn-sewn in the center of this rug. The background and the geometric and floral borders are all chenille-shirred. Made by Mary Vinton of East Braintree, Massachusetts, about 1840. Size unknown. (Reproduced from *Handmade Rugs* by Ella Shannon Bowles, published by Little, Brown & Co., 1927. Then in the collection of Mrs. Elizabeth H. Russell.)

33 (above), 33a (opposite, above). The Caswell Carpet, so named because it was made by Zeruah Higley Guernsey Caswell, is one of the most famous and well-documented works of American rugmaking, and it is a masterpiece of American folk art. Made in Castleton, Vermont, during the 1830s, it comprises seventy-six embroidered wool squares, each of a unique design, plus a rectangular section (see detail at top of opposite page). This section covered the hearthstone in summer when the fireplace was not in use, and it could be removed in winter to protect it from flying sparks. Dated 1835. 159″ x 147″. (The Metropolitan Museum of Art)

34 (opposite, middle), 34a (below, right). Major General Henry Knox, approaching his home in Thomaston, Maine, is depicted in this rug. The rug has retained the vibrant colors of the natural-dyed, homespun, woolen yarn. The touches of elegance and the quality of the work suggest that the maker (L. C.) had the advantages of schooling in needlework and contact with the fine arts of her period. Tent-stitch embroidery. c. 1800. 28½″ x 53½″. (The Metropolitan Museum of Art; gift of Bernice Chrysler Garbisch, 1965)

35 (opposite, below). The tree and vines in this rug, composed of very fine braids, are appliquéd on a rectangular braided ground. This use of appliqué on a braided rug may very well be unique. 1840–1850. 26″ x 42½″. (George and Janet Bookman)

EMBROIDERED AND BRAIDED RUGS

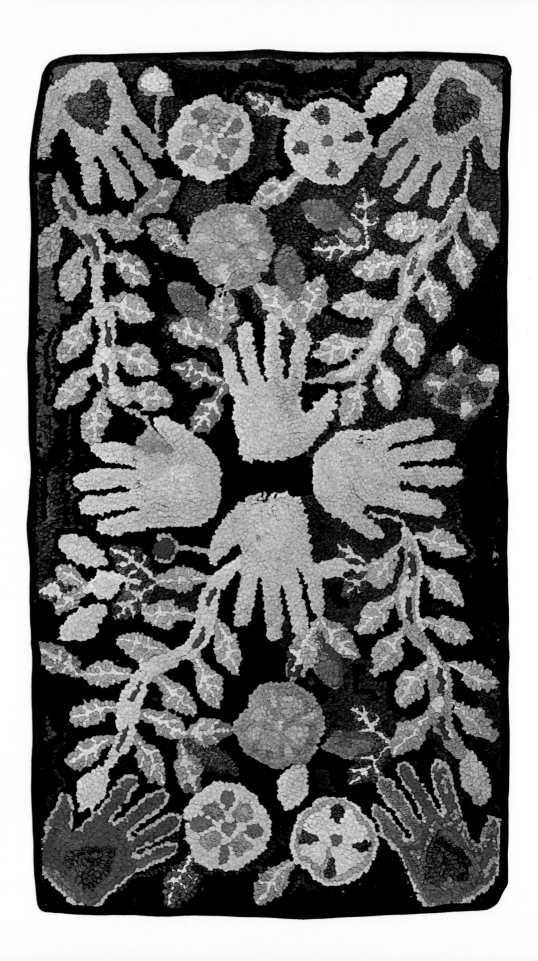

HOOKED RUGS—Part I: Nineteenth Century

By 1850 Americans had been making rugs from rags and fabric scraps for over fifty years. With a burgeoning domestic textile industry clothing was now more apt to be made from "store-bought" goods, and leftover scraps and clothing remnants could be utilized in a variety of rugmaking techniques that had become popular during the first half of the century.

Woven-rag carpets and braided rugs both used cloth strips. Later, shirring techniques developed and pictorial rugs were created with small strips and patches of cloth. The first hooked rugs were probably made in the late 1840s with linen, tow,[9] and homespun hemp used as the foundation fabrics. The concept of pulling fabric strips *up through* a woven foundation was undoubtedly influenced by the thin hooklike device used by Americans in tambour work[10] from about 1780 to 1860. It has also been suggested that during the first half of the nineteenth century sailors and their wives may have invented the simple hooking technique. Sailors had a marlinespike tool that was used for ropework. It is similar to a rug hook, and it seems likely that a modified version of this tool was used to pull rag strips up through a woven foundation fabric.

Early attempts at hooking with a linen or hemp foundation were apparently not satisfying to rugmakers. Very few rugs with a linen or hemp base are extant, probably because the relatively tight weave of these fabrics made the pulling through of fabric strips difficult and time-consuming.

It was the introduction of jute burlap (i.e. gunny-sacking, hessian cloth) that made the hooking technique popular and practical in North America. The loose open weave of burlap and the strength of the jute fiber were quickly recognized by rugmakers to constitute an ideal base for hooked rugs. Jute fiber was introduced to Europe from India around 1820. Samples of jute were sent from India to the textile mills at Dundee, Scotland, where experiments were conducted to adapt this new, cheap fiber to the manufacture of a base for commercial carpets. The experiments proved successful and by 1833 machinery in British mills that had been used for weaving flax into carpet base began being converted to accept jute. In 1838 the Dutch started converting from flax to jute for the sacking of coffee exported from their colonies in the East Indies and by 1850 the British were producing jute sacking in quantity at the mills in Scotland. Between 1854 and 1857 English-made, steam-driven machines were installed in the factories in Calcutta, India. European textile mills could not compete with the newly mechanized Indian jute industry with its advantages of cheaper labor and local raw materials.

36 (opposite). This powerful rug contains motifs that are used with unusual folkloric symbolism. Four hands, each containing a pale heart, radiate from the center, while the hands that reach in from the corners have dark gray hearts. The foliage not only functions as a decorative background, but also connects one of the central hands to a corresponding hand in each corner, for the vines seem to grow out of or into each of the hands. The heart-in-the-hand motif is a symbol of the Odd Fellows fraternal order, and this symbol appears on a wide range of handmade objects from quilts to cookie molds. In this rug the heart in the hand seems to be used as a kind of mystical statement. The modern Russian artist, Marc Chagall, whose paintings frequently contain folklore symbolism, used a similar heart-in-the-hand motif in his painting, *Paris Through the Window*. New Jersey. c. 1875. 38″ x 22″.

38 (below), 38a (opposite). This piece, hooked on a linen base, bears an overall similarity to many yarn-sewn designs. The clean, sparse quality of the composition is enlivened by details such as the date inscribed on the flower bowl, a different tilt to each of the stars, and a hummingbird drawing nectar from a rose. Dated 1858. 26″ x 69″. (Jane Gair)

37 (opposite, above). There are a number of reasons that lead us to believe this is one of the earliest existing examples of rug hooking. The foundation is, to our knowledge, unique. Homespun hemp was painstakingly adapted into an open basket weave by pulling three threads and leaving three threads alternately throughout the warp (length) and the weft (width) of the foundation. The fabric strips are cut from early home-dyed, homespun woolens, and the hooking of such thick material results in a dense ribboned texture. The overall design, uncluttered line, purity of the stylized forms, and particularly the border give it the look of yarn-sewn rugs. A patriotic sentiment has been harmonized within a floral motif by transforming the central flower into a simplified American shield. This early experiment in hooking was regarded as one of the most important rugs of the C. M. Traver Collection that was sold at auction in 1925. c. 1840. 57" x 75". (Joseph and Ellen Wetherell)

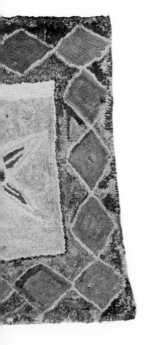

India soon dominated the world market in the production of burlap (and still does today), particularly in the cheaper rough materials such as sacking. These technological advancements were in large measure responsible for burlap sacking becoming commonplace in North America by the late 1850s.

Hooked rugs have been called "America's one indigenous folk art."[11] Both as a technique and as a means of artistic expression, it was in America (including both the United States and Canada) that this rugmaking technique was conceived and developed. The long-held supposition (championed by William Kent in the 1930s) that these rugs were of British derivation has been challenged by textile and rug authorities. Marius Barbeau in "The Origin of the Hooked Rug,"[12] Ella Shannon Bowles in *Homespun Handicrafts*,[13] Virginia D. Parslow (Partridge) in *The Concise Encyclopedia of American Antiques*,[14] Allen Eaton in *Handicrafts of the Southern Highlands*,[15] Waugh and Foley in *Collecting Hooked Rugs*,[16] Lydia Le Baron Walker in *Homecraft Rugs*,[17] and many others state their belief that the rug-hooking craft was indigenous to North America. The most convincing proof for this theory is the nonexistence of early examples of hooked rugs or of literature and records about hooking in museums and private collections in Great Britain.

In England and Scotland techniques for making mats and rugs from fabric remnants had developed as early as 1800.[18] Derived from the ancient technique of thrumming,[19] the British made "pegged" and "brodded" rugs by poking small fabric pieces through a woven cloth foundation. These English rugs have been confused with hooked rugs, although they are rarely pictorial and even the geometric designs tend to have a central medallion rather than an overall pattern. They also are easily identified by their very shaggy rag surface and by the dotted clumps of fabric that appear on the reverse side of these rugs.

Hooked rugs were made in England at the end of the nineteenth century. This was well after hooking had become popular in the United States and Canada. Most nineteenth-century English hooked rugs were much influenced by the commercial patterns that were manufactured in America. The English became aware of these stamped burlap designs through advertisements by pattern manufacturers that appeared in American magazines. Mail-order firms such as Sears Roebuck and Montgomery Ward offered patterns in their catalogues in the 1890s (see page 81), many of which reached England.

Hooked rugs were first made in Maine, New Hampshire, the Maritime Provinces of Canada (New Brunswick, Nova Scotia, and Prince Edward Island) as well as Labrador, Newfoundland, and areas of French Quebec. By the 1860s the craft had spread all through New

39 (above). This rug very probably contains the earliest date on a hooked rug that is contemporary to the piece. It was made by Ellen McKeever of Merrimack, New Hampshire, when she was 23. Her use of a specific day of the month suggests that it commemorates some special event, perhaps her engagement (she was married in 1857). Dated 1856. 39″ x 57″. (Private collection)

40 (left). It is extremely unusual to find a rug's locale incorporated into its design. The scalloped vine border, the subjects of house, bird, tree, eagle, and flower vase represent a cross section of favorite rugmaking design motifs successfully combined within one piece. Made by Abigail Smith, New Maryland, Nova Scotia. Dated 1860. Size unknown. Reproduced from The Magazine *Antiques*, August 1947.

41 (left, below). The bird within the central oval adds exceptional interest to the genteel formality of this floral rug. c. 1860. 54¾″ x 29½″. (The Henry Francis du Pont Winterthur Museum)

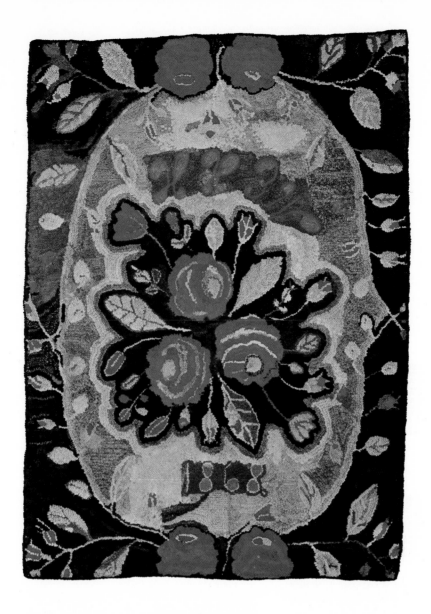

42 (above). A spray of flowers spreads from the center of this rug, determining the outward movement of the entire design. The letters of the signature, M. E. H. N., and the numerals of the date have been rendered in terms both of color and of calligraphy to work as an integral part of the overall pattern. Dated 1868. 46" x 32½".

43 (left). Floral rugs often feature a vase or bowl. This rug uses a massive cabbage rose with its leaves as a base. The cream-colored background intensifies the silhouettes and also indicates that this rug was probably intended as a showpiece and was used in a spot where it would receive little wear. 1865–1875. 41" x 52". (Joseph and Ellen Wetherell)

44 (above). A rather tame and comfortable-looking leopard is surrounded here by a meandering, flowering vine of remarkable variety. The style of the flowers and the fringed edges are reminiscent of earlier rugs. c. 1865. 34½″ x 67½″. (Private collection)

45 (below), 45a (opposite, left). Hearts, anchors, and stars are design elements often found in the folk art made by nineteenth-century sailors. In the detail opposite (fig. 45a) we can see the perforations caused by pulling thick fabric strips through a tightly woven linen base. c. 1850. 21″ x 30″. (Photograph courtesy Hovey and Evelyn Gleason)

England and the Atlantic seacoast, as well as into parts of Pennsylvania. Later, toward the end of the nineteenth century, hooked rugs were made throughout America. Whether the first hooked rug was made in Canada or in the United States is debatable and academic, since during the nineteenth century the area of Maine and the Maritime Provinces was really one continuous region in spite of a national boundary line.

The commerce and culture of both parts of the region were homogeneous. The people shared the same climate, many of the same industries, and the same national origins (Scotch, English, Irish, and German). The region consisted of many small towns and fishing villages where winters were hard and conditions were quite primitive. Such Victorian luxuries as manufactured carpets were rare and greatly treasured. The irresistible opportunity to simulate this luxury with a homemade equivalent was provided by the availability of burlap, salvaged at no cost from sacking, and of scraps of discarded clothing. This region was the major source of hooked rugs in the nineteenth century, and the making of these rugs later became a cottage industry that would contribute an important source of revenue to many households in the

46 (above) This curly-tailed mongrel is depicted as the king of his barnyard paradise. He is surrounded by an assortment of friends, including a squirrel, several cats, and a bird who hovers protectively above him, its tiny wings outstretched like those of a majestic eagle. c. 1870. 28½″ x 42″. (The Barenholtz Collection)

47 (right). These wonderfully stylized, fat-chested roosters have been given distinctively different personalities. One rooster is turned sideways, implying that the rug was composed to be enjoyed from several directions. c. 1865. 58½″ x 34″. (Mr. and Mrs. Edwin Braman)

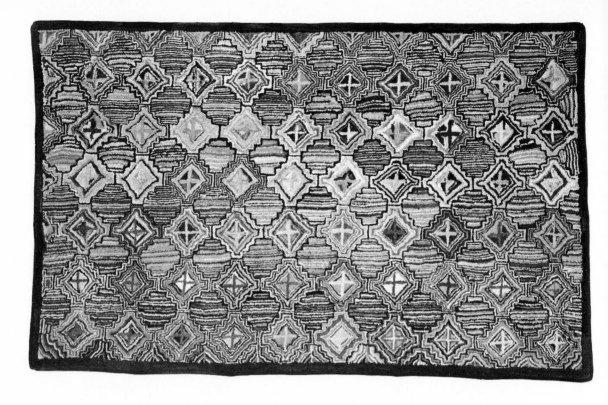

48 (above). The eccentric execution of a basic pattern has produced here a quivering optical effect, compelling the eye to travel between geometry and detail. c. 1885. 52″ x 85½″. (Dalmar A. Tifft)

49 (below). A kaleidoscopic star is highlighted by a marbleized diamond grid. c. 1885. 21″ x 38″.

area. For the seafaring people of the Northeast, winters had always been spent in making and repairing nets and sails, and men, women, and children worked at homecrafts during the evenings and during the snowbound winter months when neither fishing nor farming was possible. The skill needed for hooking rugs came quite naturally, and its popularity spread throughout the northeastern seacoast.

Dated examples of any craft are always a great help to collectors and researchers. In the case of hooked rugs the presence of a date is not always conclusive, since there appears to have been a custom of including anniversary or commemorative dates on hooked rugs. We know of several rugs with eighteenth-century dates that have burlap foundations indicating that they were made in the second half of the nineteenth century and the fabrics were clearly of nineteenth- or even twentieth-century origin. We have illustrated a bold, well-designed rug dated 1841. The base is burlap and the fabrics and aniline dyes lead us to believe that the rug was made around 1890, probably to commemorate a fiftieth anniversary. Such obviously important historical dates as 1776 should be viewed with suspicion. Dated rugs that portray personalities, ships, and famous houses or places

50 (above). This rugmaker used subtle striations to achieve delicate movement within the field of clover shapes. c. 1880. 38½" x 47¼". (George E. Schoellkopf Gallery)

51 (left). Brilliant color pulsates here within a network of freely drawn diamonds. 1885–1895. 31" x 66". (Beatrice Shilstone)

are likely to have been made well after the person, place, or event had become legendary. *The presence of burlap is almost a certain indication of a post-1850 date.* The rug in figure 40, dated June 10, 1856, is the earliest accurately dated hooked rug we know of. It also appears to be one of the first rugs to be hooked on burlap. Rugs hooked on linen or hemp are usually pre-1860, but the base material is not in itself conclusive. The general style of design as well as the types of fabrics used and the colors (natural versus aniline dyes) often give a more exact determination of the date. The making of hooked rugs during the nineteenth century was apparently not thought to be of importance as art[20] or even as a needlecraft. Nearly nothing was written about hooking in such ladies' fashion and needlework magazines as *Godey's Lady's Book* and *Peterson's Monthly Magazine*. Hooked-rug making was considered a country craft, and the rugs were not thought to be suitable for fashionable Victorian homes. Nineteenth-century publications did carry ads for patterns and mechanical hooking devices (figs. 118 and 119).

52 (above), 52a, 52b (left). Hooked rugs were generally made to be seen by family and friends and often contained familiar images and details. Behind many pieces of first-rate folk art lies a personal story, a fragment of life that is very often lost to us. Fortunately, in the case of this rug we know a bit of the story. The figures portrayed are Almon Smith and Lydia Furlong, and the date of their wedding, Nov. 25, 1866, has been included although it is not visible in this photograph. At the time Almon Smith was running an inn in Limerick, Maine. The rug was bought from Smith's widow, a second wife, whom he was said to have acquired through a newspaper advertisement. c. 1875. 65″ x 77″. (New Hampshire Historical Society)

53 (left). Geometric patterns like this did not require drawing skill, but provided a vehicle for rugmakers with graphic talent to create aesthetic abstractions. This pattern gives the subtle optical illusion of bulging from the center. The vitality associated with folk art emerges in the erratic and expressive centers of the stars. c. 1875. 28½" x 37".

54 (below). The star and tulips, distinctive Pennsylvania motifs, have been combined here in an unusual radial arrangement. The fields of the central square and corner triangles are broken with unpredictable strokes of light and dark. c. 1880. 29" x 41". (Steven and Helen Kellogg)

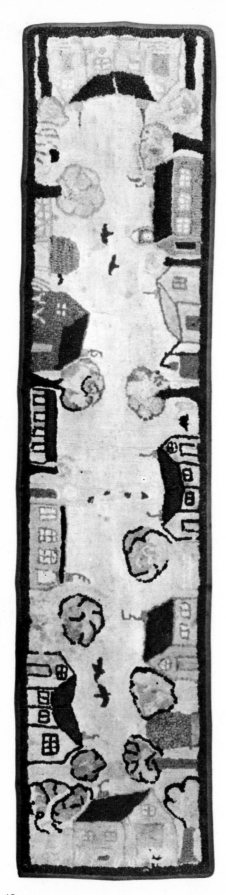

The hooking technique itself is quite simple. A ten-inch to twelve-inch strip of cloth[21] is held beneath a woven foundation (usually burlap), and a hook is inserted through an opening on the surface and a loop of the cloth strip is pulled up through it. The hook is then inserted into an adjacent hole and an additional loop is pulled up; the closer the loops, the tighter the pile. After the hooking is completed, the loops are often clipped, sometimes at varying heights.

The underside of a hooked rug has loops pulled flat against the base, covering most of the foundation but leaving very small areas of the burlap showing. The reverse side of the rug repeats the design on the front. (Diagrams of the hooking technique, showing clipping as well as the reverse side of a hooked rug, are on pages 122–123.)

The many basic crafts so closely connected with these rugs, such as spinning, dyeing, weaving, sewing, and hooking itself, show the technical skills that are involved in making these rugs. The art, however, is in the design and the use of color.

In choosing a design, rugmakers seemed to be most comfortable with familiar forms. Animals, houses, and flowers were the most popular motifs. People, ships, and landscapes required more skill and appear less frequently. Often, a member of the family or a talented friend would draw in the design and the actual hooking might be done by one or several members of the family. The design was frequently drawn on the burlap with the charred end of a stick or even a piece of charcoal from the fireplace. Geometric designs obviously required less drawing skill and sometimes even quilt patterns were used. Circular motifs were formed by overlapping tracings of a drinking glass or saucer, while ruled, straight lines and square grids could be used in infinite variations. Geometric designs, which are not confined by specific line and color repetition, have the same quality of individual expression found in pictorial rugs. It is in these geometric rugs that strong, emotional feelings are conveyed through color and line abstraction. It might be noted that these geometrics were produced long before the advent of formal, non-objective art in the twentieth century. These naïve artists understood instinctively that the combination of simple basic forms, together with strong color variation could express emotion and rhythmic movements within their rugs.

55 (left). Gravity has been sacrificed for the sake of the design in this runner. Despite the fact that this New England town scene has been turned outside-in, care has still been taken to include such realistic details as a beehive, a well, and birds flying in the narrow strip of sky. c. 1880. 70″ x 16″. (Penelope Comfort Starr)

56 (above), 57 (below), 58 (overleaf). Lucy Barnard of Dixfield Common, Maine, hooked three extraordinary rugs depicting a large white house on a hill with outbuildings and stables attached. The scene in figure 57 would seem to be the earliest of the three, for Lucy still retains the traditional hooked-rug device of using a floral border to contain the house and its grounds. In figure 58 the oval border has been replaced by a spectacular rainbow, which serves to contain and shelter the house while adding to the wonderland atmosphere where flowers tower over a tiny couple canoeing on a walrus-shaped lake. In another version with a more naturalistic landscape (fig. 56), the house takes second place to Lucy's favorite horse, which we know was named Betsy. c. 1860. Fig. 56: 36″ x 65″. Fig. 57: 30½″ x 60″. Fig. 58: 29″ x 60″. (The Metropolitan Museum of Art; Sansbury Mills Fund, 1961)

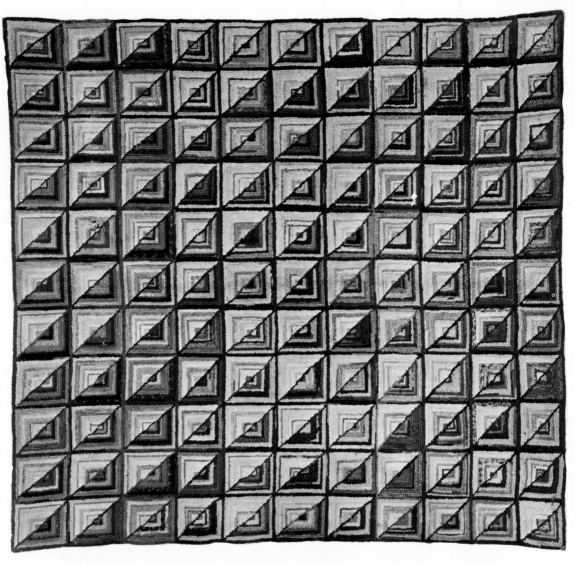

The color range in these rugs was as varied as any painter's palette. In earlier times rugmakers extracted their dyes from native woods, plants, and berries, as well as such exotic substances as cochineal and fustic. Later, synthetic dyes expanded the color range. Rugmakers displayed their talents not only in combining colors, but also in creating them. Variation in the shades of a color could be achieved with numerous dyeing techniques. After dyeing, the cloth was cut into strips and tied into small bundles. The opportunity to draw on a variety of shades gave the gifted maker a freedom to create striated backgrounds and tonal changes in the subject. Outlines and backgrounds filled in with static color lack the vitality and feeling that many exceptional rugs possess.

The makers wanted their rugs to be attractive and pleasing, and it is logical to assume that hooking would not have become so widespread and varied in the nineteenth century had it not been for the appreciation and imitation by neighbors and friends. In our technological age it is sometimes hard to relate to the time when pride in workmanship and a desire to make common objects beautiful pervaded and influenced American life. People shared their skills and showed off their work at communal gatherings. Local fairs, sewing and quilting bees, barn raisings, and just plain get-togethers with family and friends afforded opportunities to see and show the results of their creative labor.

Many hooked rugs have the virtues of primitive paintings: uninhibited designs and perspectives, bold and unconventional use of color, and inventiveness and broad artistic license when attempting complex or detailed subjects. The making of a rug required skill and patience, and often personal details were given inordinate attention and styled with wry humor. These rugs have the virtue of usually disregarding professional artistic standards, since they were made to be used and enjoyed by the maker and her family and friends.

Rugmaking by relaxed, nonprofessional artisans continued to be an important expression of American folk art during the twentieth century. Rugs made after 1900 are illustrated and discussed in the second part of this chapter (page 87).

62 (below). The inner rectangle of this bright geometric rug is hooked and the wide border is composed of raveled-knit shirring, which give it a deep shaggy texture. Reds, blues, browns, and whites dominate, and in the border the random-appearing patches of color are actually organized around a rather free checkerboard pattern. 1875–1885. 20½" x 37".

59 (opposite, above). Strong diagonal lines emphasize the division of light and dark tones within this Log Cabin pattern. The tonal variation produces an effect of light and shadow falling across a wafflelike grid. c. 1880. 70" x 78". (Jonathan Holstein and Gail van der Hoof)

60 (opposite, below). The focal point of this piece, a thick volume probably representing a family Bible, is rendered in perspective within a bordered ground of flat ornamental flowers. 1870–1880. 29" x 46½". (Mr. and Mrs. Ben Mildwoof)

61 (right, above). An extremely geometric vision of a flower vase works beautifully with a purely abstract chevron border. 1880–1890. 45" x 36". (Photograph courtesy Sotheby Parke Bernet Inc.)

63 (opposite). A glass dome protects the flowers in a large ornamental urn set on a pedestal. It is placed side by side with weedlike wild flowers in an environment made even more enigmatic by a wriggling garden snake and symbolic stars and crescent moons. Made by John Filker, Amherst, Ohio. Dated 1877. 48″ x 34″. (Mr. and Mrs. Richard Bury)

65 (below). The design of this rug was clearly influenced by cotton crazy quilts. The repetition of strong motifs such as the stars and moon even mimics the scattered use of the same fabric characteristic of patchwork quilts. This rugmaker used her imagination further to invent the fabric patterns as well as the way they fit together. 1870–1880. 40″ x 50″. (Private collection)

64 (above). This rug has borrowed motifs from Victorian embroidered silk and velvet quilts: the fan-shaped corner devices, appliquéd, figurative medallion, and embroiderylike lines of the floral vines. c. 1875. 38″ x 46″. (George E. Schoellkopf Gallery)

66 (above). This unusually large rug measures 7' x 9' and was probably made for a Masonic lodge. The central field is filled with well-known Masonic symbols such as the compass, trowel, and all-seeing eye. The face on the full moon adds a whimsical touch to the symbolism and the letters *C. H. F.*, framed by a ladder, may have been the rugmaker's initials. Reproduced from an advertisement by Mrs. Edward O. Schernikow in *The Antiquarian*, August 1930. Present owner unknown.

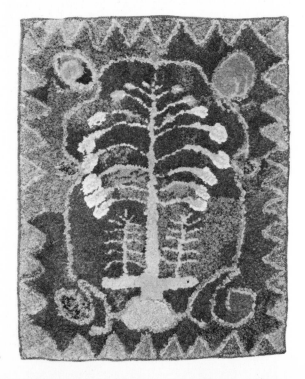

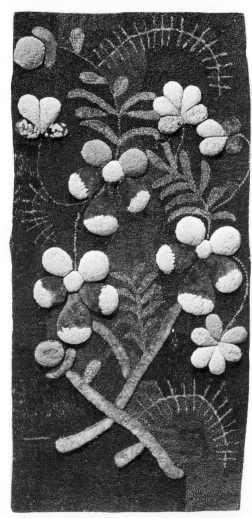

67 (opposite, left). A tree of life spreads its branches over two spindly seedlings. 1870–1880. 35½″ x 28½″.

68 (opposite, right). The technique of clipping and forming the pile of a rug into three-dimensional forms gives the petals and stems in this "Waldoboro-type"[22] rug a full bas-relief quality. Arching skeletal fronds provide a delicate contrast to the major motifs. c. 1870. 38″ x 19″. (William C. Putnam and Beverly T. Smith)

69 (above). Geometric stars with their satellites, and a red moon—in full and in crescent—form an explosive galaxy. The turbulence of the background adds an almost apocalyptic mood. c. 1880. 31″ x 52″.

70 (below). The choice of deep blue for the windows of this house contributes an aura of mystery to the distinctive mood conveyed by this rug. The house is set among abstract streaks that have the quality of agitated brushwork. c. 1880. 35½″ x 58½″.

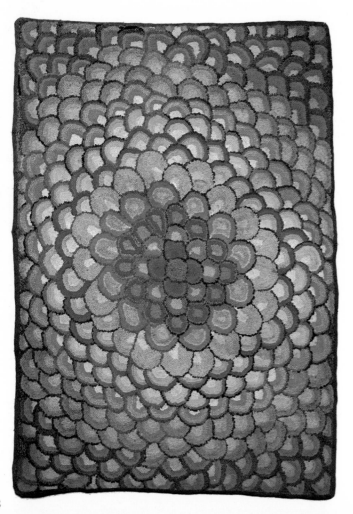

71 (opposite, above). The "Waldoboro" technique has been carried to its ultimate in this rug in which the pile of the dog's body is almost three inches deep. This luxurious texture gives realistic depth to the anatomy of this Dalmatian and a naturalistic shagginess to his coat. 1865–1875. 31″ x 54½″. (Quintina Colio)

72 (opposite, below left). This "clamshell" pattern radiating from a central circle resembles an enormous spreading chrysanthemum. The subtle gradations in color give a full-bodied swelling effect to the "flower." c. 1880. 34″ x 50″. (Pine Cone Antiques)

73 (opposite, below right). Variations on a star shape alternate with more figurative panels in what was evidently at one time a longer runner. c. 1865. 12½″ x 47″.

74 (right, above). A variety of reds is used to give each "clamshell" form an individually shaped focal point. 1880–1890. 23″ x 37″. (Dalmar A. Tifft)

75 (right, below). This Baby Blocks pattern achieves an optically deceptive quality in which the blocks seem to shift constantly from protruding shapes to receding niches. The irregular placing of darks, lights, and halftones creates inconsistencies in the tilt of the blocks that are fascinating and unpredictable. c. 1880. 53″ x 68″. (Eliot Hubbard)

60

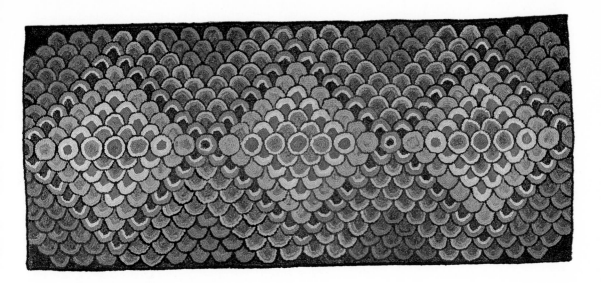

76 (opposite), 76a (right). The tapestrylike quality of this piece is achieved by repeating the same basic motifs in three horizontal panels and varying details of color within them. The middle band is a mirror image of the top and bottom panels. (A very similar design, including a delicate unicorn, is found in an early nineteenth-century embroidered carriage cushion from Sweden, which in turn is believed to have been inspired by an earlier Flemish weaving pattern.[23]) c. 1885. 57″ x 90″. (Ed and Mary Lou Jackson)

77 (above). A "clamshell" pattern of rose, blue, browns, and beiges builds outward from a central horizontal row of polka dots to achieve a composition of three bold diamonds. c. 1885. 31″ x 71″.

78 (below). The vase and spreading flower arrangement here have a rich three-dimensional surface texture produced by a pile that has been clipped and raised in the manner of "Waldoboro"-type rugs. The light markings within the dark background suggest a backdrop of draperies. c. 1875. 19″ x 36″. (George and Janet Bookman)

79 (above). The maker of this rug has taken a painter's approach to landscape and contained it within a border obviously imitating a picture frame. The scene is personalized by the details of the gazebo, a little dog in the front yard, and a toy boat floating in the pond. c. 1885. 26″ x 39½″. (Photograph courtesy Kelter-Malcé Antiques)

80 (below). This rug, made in tribute to Abraham Lincoln, is inscribed "A. L. 1809 U.S. '61–'65" (the dates of his birth and presidential terms). Lincoln's distinctive profile is seen in silhouette beside his famous log cabin. The riderless horse has a saddle trimmed in patriotic red, white, and blue, and the enigmatic owl may represent Lincoln's legendary wisdom. 1865–1875. 30″ x 45″. (Greenfield Village and Henry Ford Museum)

81 (above). This cat must have been a champion mouser, as proud of himself as his owner was. In this humorous portrait the maker has captured the individuality of the family pet with its very distinctive calico markings and striped tail. c. 1880. 28″ x 44″. (George E. Schoellkopf Gallery; photograph courtesy Gary C. Cole)

82 (below). A notable characteristic of many hooked rugs is the use of striations to give a feeling of movement to an otherwise static area. In this rug a fluid sense of motion has been given to the horse and the background. The zigzag border intensifies the sense of animation. Pennsylvania. Dated 1880. 36″ x 53″.

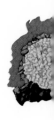

83 (top), 83a (center, above). This amazingly well-preserved rug was found wrapped in old newspapers in York, Pennsylvania. It was made in the 1890s but never used. The extraordinary brilliance of its colors gives some idea of the original intensity of many other rugs of the period. The two yellow chicks perched beak to beak on half of an eggshell form a most unusual heart motif. c. 1895. 26½" x 43". (Photograph courtesy Ronald and Marilyn Kowaleski)

84 (above). The charm and simplicity of this pair of rabbits are highlighted by the subtle abstractions against which they are set. 1800–1890. 29" x 40". (Photograph courtesy Phyllis and Sidney Rosner)

85 (center). Symmetrically facing horses are given a haloed effect by their bold double outline. Red shapes resembling hearts decorate the corners. c. 1895. 21" x 38".

86 (opposite, top). The variation of tones in both the background and the bodies of the roosters results in sophisticated nuances of abstracted color. c. 1890. 22" x 39". (Hastings House Antiques)

87 (opposite, center). Two cats with glowing eyes have been differentiated by reversing their light and dark tones. The date 1892 has been worked into the lower inner border. 20" x 29½".

88 (opposite, bottom). Four smiling rabbits anticipate the delights of the giant carrots that must lurk beneath such oversized leafy tops. 1890–1900. 31" x 53".

89 (left). Although an incongruously violent scene has been chosen for this welcome mat, it has been depicted in such a happy way that we feel welcome nevertheless. The whale has sent one boat flying, but its occupant smiles like a soaring angel. The pair of Cupid hearts suggests that the greeting was lovingly intended for a whaler's homecoming. 1890–1900. 22½″ x 31″. (Nina Howell Starr)

91 (below), 91a (opposite, below). In a scene worthy of Cinemascope a whaling ship is flanked by two small boats, one of which, with its crew, has been sent flying by a thrashing fluke. Heavy black string has been tacked to the surface of the hooking to simulate the rigging of the ship. Large harpoons add dramatic authenticity to the border, possibly indicating the influence of an experienced whaler in the designing of this piece. A rather thorough knowledge of the whaling trade is demonstrated in the detail at right (fig. 91a). A seaman is seen stripping a whale carcass of its blubber, and flames and smoke rise up from a smokestack as the blubber is rendered for its oil. c. 1890. 40″ x 104″. (Barbara Johnson)

90 (opposite, center). A dramatic, windblown effect has been achieved in the firm contours of the flag and patriotic pennant. c. 1890. 35" x 49½". (Mr. and Mrs. Peter Goodman)

92 (above). An anchor resting on what appears to be a body of water separates two houses. Horseshoes are added to the traditional nautical stars and anchors, probably as good-luck charms for the mariner away from home. Dated 1892. 24½" x 37½". (Photograph courtesy Kathy and John Schoemer)

93 (opposite). Rainbow stripes were popular among Pennsylvania quilters of the 1890s, but this is the only example we know of where they were used with such purity in a rug. This rug may well have been made by a quilter who found she could go even further with her talent for color by choosing from the endless range of commercial aniline dyes that had become readily available by that time. Vibrant colors graduate from light to dark within each broad band. The challenge of using color alone as the substance of a work has been beautifully realized. 1890–1900. 45″ x 28½″. (Jonathan Holstein and Gail van der Hoof)

94 (above). In this powerful and almost surreal still-life arrangement fruits and blossoms appear to float weightlessly around a pot of flowers. The forms are outlined with vividly contrasting colors, giving the entire composition a luminous glow. 1885–1895. 37½″ x 41½″. (Private collection)

95 (left). Part of a New England town is depicted here with almost maplike clarity. Two bold loops create a strong composition that both contains and separates the houses and the church. The special personality of this town and perhaps the rugmaker, too, emerges through a variety of details: gardens with their tottering cats, the bashful oversize horse, and the loving attention given to each doorway and window shade. 1880–1890. 27″ x 50″. (Ed and Mary Lou Jackson)

96 (opposite, below left). A house cat with expressive jagged markings finds itself afloat on a cloudlike scalloped rug. This whimsical portrait is enlivened by a frame of colored hexagons. 1875–1885. 35″ x 35″.

97 (below center). Contained within an irregular and energetic border, two fragile shorebirds approach a flower bowl of overpowering proportions. c. 1875. 33″ x 39″. (Jane Gair)

98 (below). Commercial pattern rugs featuring lions were popular in this period, but the maker of this piece evidently decided to strike out on her own and produced this startled lion in its field of daisies. c. 1890. 36″ x 40½″. (George E. Schoellkopf Gallery)

99 (above). Mrs. Eleanor Blackstone of Lacon, Illinois, hooked six extremely large rugs between 1880 and 1890, all recording events in the history of her family. Four of these have survived, and we have reproduced the three now in public collections. The extraordinary vignettes depicting Mrs. Blackstone's six children, their personalities, their pastimes, and their pets even include actual strands of their hair worked into the individual portraits. Daughters Anne and Blanche were well trained in the craft, and Blanche is believed to have had a large part in the design of all these rugs. This rug is full of names, dates, and inscriptions that tell something about each child. Even daughter Nellie, who died in infancy, has her portrait poignantly inscribed "Suffer little children to come unto me." c. 1885. 94" x 117". (Greenfield Village and Henry Ford Museum)

100 (left). A Blackstone family picnic complete with roasting chickens and all the fixings is spread out in the "Old Home Woo[d]s." This rug, like the other Blackstone pieces, is filled with sayings and biblical words of advice, here directed at son Roy, 20 years old. c. 1890. 111¾" x 123½". (The Metropolitan Museum of Art; gift of Bernice Chrysler Garbisch, 1963)

101 (right). Here the Blackstone clan has congregated in front of the family home on a wintry February day. The strong attachment they had for their home is reflected in the inscription "In my father's house are many mansions." These Blackstone narrative rug pictures deserve special recognition as superb American folk tapestries. Dated "Feb. 23 1890." 95" x 112½". (Greenfield Village and Henry Ford Museum)

102 (above). Simple and direct as a child's pull toy, this bright red horse is posed on a small box pedestal. The oversized head, elongated body, and delicate legs almost give the illusion of its being a horse costume containing two men. c. 1885. 21″ x 31″. (Allan L. Daniel)

103 (below). A brown and orange horse named Black Beauty trots through a garden of rectangular patches brightened by flowers and autumn leaves. c. 1885. 40″ x 98″. (Richard and Nelle Hankinson)

The details of horses on these two pages have been taken from figure 27 (page 30), figure 95 (page 71), and figure 99 (page 72).

95a

104 (right, above). A toylike pinto pony is surrounded by freely drawn cookie-cutter shapes and symbols. c. 1890. 37″ x 44″. (Burton and Helaine Fendelman)

27a

105 (right, center). The design source for this silhouetted horse was quite likely a rooftop weathervane. The angular fields of atmospheric blues and beiges form a background suggesting the wind's direction. c. 1885. 23½″ x 43″. (Photograph courtesy Mr. and Mrs. Burt Purmell)

99a

106 (right, below). A high-spirited pony is outlined against a conglomeration of stars, leaves, and animals. The little dog at bottom center appears to be barking loudly at the horse. 1870–1880. 31″ x 48″. (Ron and Anita Klink)

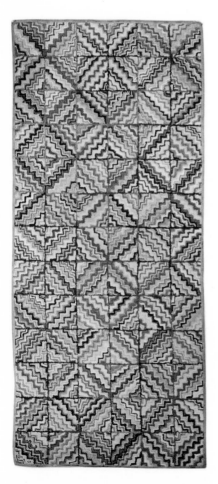

107 (above). An unusually delicate geometric effect is achieved by contrasting subtle pastel hues against alternate black and purple squares. The absence of rigid geometric repetition creates a gentle movement between light and dark. c. 1890. 25½″ x 35″. (Dalmar A. Tifft)

108 (left). Composed of many different colors and woven pattern scraps, this geometric design is sometimes referred to as the Wave and Stepped pattern. c. 1890. 70″ x 31½″.

109 (below). Vivid colors and deep contrasts of tone distinguish this rug, which is designed like a Straight Furrow Log Cabin quilt. c. 1880. 49″ x 34″. (Barbara Johnson)

110 (above). In this winter scene the town and its people have been captured with the "stop-action" quality sometimes found in photographs. Horse-drawn sleighs move out in all directions, emphasizing the receding depth of the townscape; one horse has even traveled halfway out of the picture, which is a very unusual compositional device for a rugmaker. c. 1890. 34" x 58½". (Timothy and Pamela Hill)

111 (below). A flower arrangement in an oddly scalloped vase is set on a mat suspended like a flying carpet. The striped border gives the look of a framed picture. c. 1890. 39" x 57¼". (Private collection)

112 (above). This bowl of flowers has been given an incongruous touch by the two fish this float between the corner hearts. Dated 1896. 33½" x 50". (Silver Spring Farm Antiques)

113 (left). Hearts were among the favorite decorative motifs in rugmaking. Here they are used plentifully and appropriately to celebrate Saint Valentine's Day. c. 1885. 28½" x 36½". (Herbert W. Hemphill, Jr.)

114 (below). Dates worked into hooked rugs are not necessarily conclusive evidence of when a rug was made. In this case the burlap base, the colors, and the fabrics lead us to believe that this rug was made in the 1890s. The 1841 dating suggests that the piece commemorates an anniversary. (Betty Sterling)

Shaker communities were established and active throughout
the United States from about 1800 to 1900. The Shakers lived
according to rigid and specific religious beliefs and purpose-
ful labor and meticulous craftsmanship were part of their
credo. The Shakers reduced design in their craftwork to its
purest and most practical form, which developed into a distinctive and much-admired style in furniture, woodwork,
boxes, and baskets—all beautiful in their simplicity and excellent in their workmanship. Most Shaker rugs are characterized
by geometric designs and multiple borders, with braided
edges added for durability. We have illustrated rare examples
of figural imagery, all made at the Pleasant Hill Shaker
Community in Harrodsburg, Kentucky, at the end of the
nineteenth century.

117 (below). Simple flowers and a four-pointed star are set
against sweeping fields of color. c. 1880. 29″ x 73″.
(Shakertown, Pleasant Hill, Kentucky, Inc.)

115 (top). The spare outline of this
running horse with a touch of red in
its tongue represents, in our opinion,
primitive form at its best. The horse
appears to be spotlighted by dazzling
multiple borders that are both hooked
and braided. c. 1880. 37″ x 41″.
(Shakertown, Pleasant Hill, Kentucky,
Inc.)

116 (above). An almost electric
combination of border within border
and a scalloped inner field enclose
the word GOOD, a strong reminder
of that simple virtue. c. 1880.
22″ x 36″. (Shakertown, Pleasant Hill,
Kentucky, Inc.)

PATTERNS

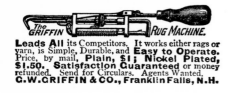

118 (top). Advertisement in *Lippincott's Monthly Magazine*, 1887.

119 (above). Advertisement in *Scribner's Magazine*, 1889.

120 (below). Edward Sands Frost pattern, Spaniel. c. 1890. (Private collection)

Much has already been written about Edward Sands Frost the Maine tin peddler who cut designs into metal stencils, and then used them to stamp patterns on burlap for hooked rugs. Between 1864 and 1876 he sold these hand-colored patterns to housewives along his peddling route. Frost's designs are characterized by stiffly posed animals surrounded by very organized geometric or floral borders. One of Frost's most popular designs is this spaniel (fig. 120). Other popular animal patterns include stags, several horses (one includes a large potted sunflower and a water pump), a Dalmatian, a cat-and-kitten welcome rug, an eagle and shield, and two ducks with foliage. In addition to dozens of floral designs—most of them with balanced, oval floral centers and floral borders—there is a pattern containing a central shield and the words "Centennial 1776–1876."

Frost also made patterns with Masonic and fraternal emblems centered within a floral border. In addition, there are dozens of "Oriental" style Frost patterns.

In 1886 Ebenezer Ross of Toledo, Ohio, invented a mechanical "punch-hook,"[24] and to help facilitate its sale, he published a catalogue in 1891 that contained fifty-six colored prints offering for sale rug patterns that were to be made with his hook. Most of the patterns were copies of Frost's designs, but the Lion and Palm (fig. 121) and the Mastiff Dog (fig. 129) are probably Ross originals. Later, mail-order firms such as Montgomery Ward manufactured patterns that copied both Frost and Ross.

The earliest rug patterns were probably those made in Lowell, Massachusetts, in the 1850s by the firm of Chambers and Lealand. They specialized in stamped embroidery patterns, but they also produced large printing blocks made of wood with inlaid copper designs that were stamped with a dye solution on burlap or linen. These pattern blocks were purchased by Philena Moxley in 1876. She greatly expanded the line of hooked rug designs. Most of these large hooked rug blocks were used as firewood during a coal strike many years later and only a few still survive. These are on display along with rugs made from them at the Wenham Historical Society in Wenham, Massachusetts.

In 1899 the Diamond Dye Company, recognizing that most rugmakers home-dyed their cloth before hooking, published a booklet that gave instructions for rug hooking and offered patterns and rug hooks for sale by mail. In the 1930s Ralph Burnham and Co. sold a line of rug patterns that were copies of early rugs.

Patterns are an interesting facet of hooked-rug making, but while they may have helped to popularize the craft, they stifled the originality and spontaneity that are essential to great hooked rugs in particular and folk art in general.

121, 122, 123 (left). The finest and one of the most popular commercial patterns was the Lion and Palm by Ebenezer Ross (fig. 121). Rug hookers frequently improvised on the pattern to give their work individuality. They took liberties with color, dropped borders, and even added or subtracted details as in figure 123, where the lion cub has been left out. Fig. 121: 1880–1900. (Mr. and Mrs. David Bakalar). Fig. 122: 1880–1900. Photograph courtesy George E. Schoellkopf Gallery. (Private collection). Fig. 123: 1880–1900. (Mr. and Mrs. Robert Becker)

124 (left, bottom). The maker of this rug obviously admired Ross's Lion and Palm pattern, but preferred to draw her own freehand copy. The result is expressive and naïve, especially as seen in the faces of the animals. c. 1890. (Brown-Trump Farm)

125 (above). Portion of the page of rug patterns in Montgomery Ward's catalogue for 1887.

126 (above). A particularly spry pug overlaps an irregular broad border. The date 1898 and ribbonlike initials on the sides work decoratively within the lively linework. 23″ x 40½″.

127 (below). A pair of barking dogs stand guard beside a fruit tree. The birds, each with a wriggling worm in its beak, are obviously undeterred. 1870–1880. 39″ x 61″. (Joseph and Ellen Wetherell)

The details of dogs on the opposite page have been taken from figure 33 (page 34) and figure 99 (page 72).

128 (right). A dog with a distinctive sickle-shaped tail is placed against a speckled ground that suggests falling snow. An inventive combination of checkerboard blocks and half-circles makes an exceptionally graphic border. 1880–1890. 32″ x 38½″. (George E. Schoellkopf Gallery)

33a

129 (right). Although commercial patterns often stifled originality, there are instances when an individual rugmaker has taken a commercial pattern, such as this dog produced by E. Ross and Co., and done something special with it. The striping of the dog's body and the background have a life of their own, and the dog's red harness stands out dramatically. c. 1890. 34¾″ x 54″. (George E. Schoellkopf Gallery)

99b

130 (right). Dynamic striations in the background and the body of this running setter intensify the sense of action. 1880–1890. 34½″ x 54½″. (George E. Schoellkopf Gallery)

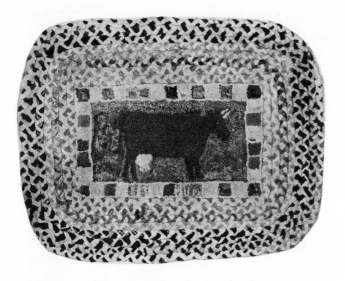

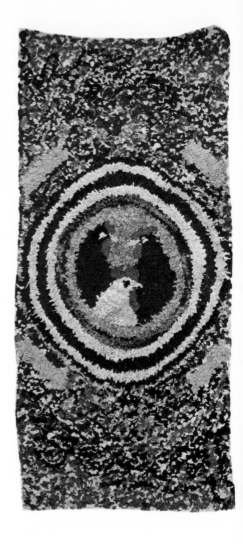

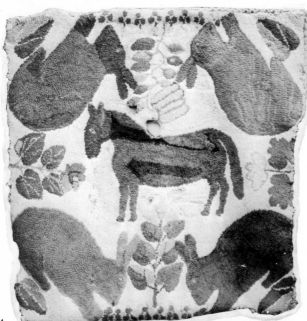

131 (left, above). An unusually wide border of braided cotton homespun frames a hooked-rug portrait of an utterly improbable barn-red cow. c. 1875. 30″ x 39″. (The Newark Museum)

132 (left, center). One waddling duck follows the other across a field of subtle browns and beiges. A few unexpected dark strokes break the background, creating the impression of movement. c. 1875. 17½″ x 22″. (Photograph courtesy James Kronen Gallery)

133 (left, below). A primitive horse is surrounded by enormous rabbits that serve as bold corner motifs. c. 1880. 33″ x 33″. (Douglas Leroy Joslin)

134 (above). The concentric arrangement of three rooster heads creates an inner ring within an unusual bull's-eye frame. c. 1885. 17½″ x 39″.

135 (above). The outline of this galloping horse may possibly have been drawn with a paper stencil, but the perception of a naïve artist has placed the horse's large eye well back of its ear. Striations have been organized into currents and whirlpools of vibrant color. c. 1880. 28½″ x 41″. Photograph courtesy Kelter-Malcé Antiques. (James Crawford)

136 (below). Care has been taken to indicate the rippling muscles of this horse, which was obviously a champion jumper. c. 1880. 34½″ x 66″. (Burton and Helaine Fendelman)

137, 138. It is always interesting to see different treatments of the same subject. Harness racing, long a popular and exciting sport in America, is shown here in two rugs with horses going full speed. In one rug the trotter is sheltered under a rainbow for good luck and in the other the driver is cheered on as if by an enthusiastic spectator to "Let Her Go."

137 (above). 1880–1890. 23" x 36". (Monique Knowlton)

138 (below). 1890–1910. 31" x 50". (Hastings House Antiques)

HOOKED RUGS—Part II: Twentieth Century

139 (above). An optical illusion is achieved in this rug with its superb geometric purity. The white diamond with its powerful bull's-eye and the border of Log Cabin squares are set off by heavy accents of subtle, broken dark tones. It is interesting to observe that this rug, made at the end of the Victorian era, deals successfully with some of the same artistic concepts explored by the Minimal artists of the 1960s. Found in Pennsylvania. 1890–1900. 29″ x 40″.

During the twentieth century hooked-rug making developed into a cottage industry in many parts of the United States and Canada. These cottage industries were frequently started where the craft was known and where there was a need among the local residents for an additional source of income. The most famous of these cottage industries was the Grenfell Mission of Labrador. The distinctive Grenfell rugs are illustrated on pages 92–93.

At the end of the nineteenth century Alex-ander Graham Bell and his wife took up summer residence on Cape Breton Island, Nova Scotia. Mrs. Bell set about stimulating handcrafts and brought in a crafts expert named Lillian Burke. Due to Miss Burke's efforts the Cheticamp Hooked Rug Industry was established in the early part of the twentieth century. In the ensuing years the area became well known for its rugs and in 1939 *The Christian Science Monitor* reported that the Cheticamp industry was "catering to New

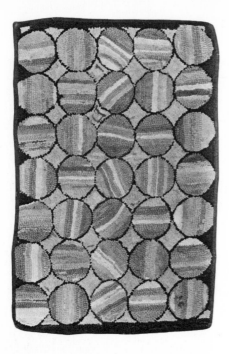

140 (above). A lively machinelike movement is achieved within a simple design by varying the tilt and angle of the stripes on the balls. 1900–1910. 36″ x 24½″.

York decorators who order rugs to be used in palatial homes." The article went on to mention that "In many homes rug earnings bring the only actual cash that is seen year round."

The cottage industry products were usually made at the workers' homes and then sold by the community organization. In many cases rugmakers worked independently and sold their rugs directly from their homes or at roadside stands. In 1928 Margaret Lathrop Law in her article, "The Hooked Rugs of Nova Scotia," wrote:

> For antique dealers, interior decorators, and summer cottagers from the States, all possessed of the hooked-mat mania, have now grown too greedy and impatient to wait for the women who a few seasons ago relied entirely on peddling their wares from door to door, or depositing them casually among the molasses and flour barrels of the village store. With characteristic American restiveness, the "go-getters" of hooked rugs having thoroughly scoured the byways of New England, now scurry in motorcars and motorboats to remote corners of Nova Scotia and Cape Breton. . . . Now there are many orders for copies of [early] rugs till recently considered secondary in value to new oilcloth. . . . In the villages of Nova Scotia to-day you can still buy rugs from fifty cents to fifty dollars, the average ranging from four to twelve dollars according to size, design, material, and, above all, value set by the individual hooker. . . . Some women never see the actual cash, for at the very store which sells their rugs, they turn the profit into food. . . . Of course, there are both women and children who make these rugs because it amuses them, and who do not actually need the money, but these are few.[25]

The cottage industry in hooked rugs was not exclusively Canadian. In 1902 Lucy Thomson founded the Subbekakasheny Industry in Belchertown, Massachusetts. The rugs made there featured designs based on American Indian motifs. The famous Abnakee hooked rugs were the products of a community enterprise founded early in the twentieth century by Helen Albee at Pequaket, New Hampshire. Named for the Abnaqui Indians, these rugs were also inspired by the American Indian rugs that were so popular then. The Abnakee rugmakers used only new materials: unused burlap for the foundation and pure wool twill flannel for the pile, which was often clipped. In 1923 the South End Home Industry was started in Boston. Facilities and supplies were provided for individuals who came during the day and made

141 (left). Letters and initials, often crudely formed and abbreviated, are a common occurrence in rugs. In many cases we can only guess at the meaning they had for the maker. In this example a person far more skilled in abstract design than in spelling and penmanship has created this unusual geometric composition. c. 1900. 35″ x 18½″.

142 (above). This action-packed Fourth of July picnic scene fits into the tradition of American genre painting. The rug was made by the same person who made the "Christmas Day" rug on the following page, and it includes all the mischievous merriment expected in a small town's celebration of Independence Day. The scene is rendered with warm understanding of the event, and we are told "All Had a Good Time." c. 1910. 37½" x 45½". (Shelburne Museum, Inc.)

hooked rugs. The rugmakers were paid a price per square foot for the work they produced, and the finished rugs were sold at the South End House and at shops in the area and at resorts.

The Maine Seacoast Missionary Society organized a scattered group of families along a 300-mile stretch of Maine seacoast into a small rugmaking industry in the 1920s. Individual towns and villages set up community industries in the 1920s and 1930s where hooked-rug making was an important occupation. The Society of Deerfield Industries at Deerfield, Massachusetts, was established in the 1920s. The Pine Burr Studio, a center in Apison, Tennessee, was established in 1921 for the purpose of training mountain women to make hooked rugs. Mrs. F. D. Huckabee who was the headworker and teacher of the group wrote: "I would judge that our products

are sold in most of the larger cities since the cash sales from one community in 1930 amounted to around $10,000. We have nothing that savors of factory work. Each piece is made in the home of the worker . . ."[26]

In 1922 Mr. and Mrs. George Cathey established the Blue Ridge Weavers at Tryon, North Carolina. In addition to weaving the group sold quilts and hooked rugs made in mountain homes by over one hundred workers. Other southern cottage industries that made hooked rugs were Rosemont Industries, founded in 1918 by Laura Copenhaver in Marion, Virginia; The Wooton Fireside Industries esablished at Wooton, Kentucky, in 1924; The Carcassonne Community Center at Gander, Kentucky, founded in 1925; The Shenandoah Community workers at Bird Haven, Virginia, founded in 1927; and the Asbury Tennessee Community Industry in the 1930s.

In *Handicrafts of the Southern Highlands* (1937) Allen Eaton describes how the cottage rug industry worked in that area:

Throughout the highlands rug making has come to be one of the more widely practised handicrafts. In some instances, temporary factories have been established by commercial organizations which supply all the materials, select the designs, and supervise the work usually handled on a piece basis; in others the work is taken into the homes where it is always done on a piece basis. But there are hundreds of people throughout the region who work independently of commercial agencies making their own rugs. . . . The technique of the hooked rug is not difficult to master but there is considerable variation of workmanship in the finished product. The same is true of the patterns and color combinations; one traveling through the region will see great numbers of uninteresting and mediocre rugs just as he will in sections of rural Canada.[27]

The cottage industry in hooked rugs developed in North America during the early part of the twentieth century for several reasons. More people lived in large cities, and the skills of such rural handicrafts as rugmaking were often forgotten and out of style. Manufactured carpets and linoleum were cheap, popular, and easily available. After World War I and all through the 1920s there was a rekindled interest in so-called Early American crafts. American glass, furniture, and hooked rugs were given special attention in home magazines such as *The House Beautiful*. Antiques publications such as *The Antiquarian* and the newly established The Magazine *Antiques* began to publish articles about hooked rugs. In the 1920s the skills of hooked-rug making still survived in some rural areas and especially in New England and the Maritime Provinces of Canada, where hooked rugs were first made. The collector and decorator interest in hooked rugs stimulated the creation of rugmakers' organizations. Companies who imported rugs from Canada advertised continuously in home and antiques magazines during the 1920s.

More than 2,000 hooked rugs were sold in the period from 1923 to 1929 in eight individual auction sales in New York City. For example, the Traver collecaion of fifty-six "Rare Hooked Rugs" was sold in 1925 (three rugs from this sale are illustrated in figs. 8, 30, and 37). In three separate auctions in 1924, 1925, and 1929, 545 rugs belonging to Mrs. Edward O. Schernikow were sold. (One of these "hooked" rugs was a bed rug dated 1819.) A collection of 460 rugs belonging to James L. Hutchinson was sold in 1927. According to the catalogue of the Anderson Galleries in New York, the Hutchinson rugs had been found "on his latest cruise to villages along the New England coast." A group of 275 "early colonial hooked rugs" owned by J. W. T. Wettleson was sold at the Anderson Galleries in 1924 (one of these rugs is illustrated in fig. 61). In two individual sales in 1923 James Shoemaker disposed of a collection of 665 rugs that he had collected over the previous fifteen years. These sales reflected the high degree of interest in hooked rugs during the 1920s.

In 1928, an old rugmaker in Nova Scotia who had hooked a black cat on a crimson background told a visitor how the rug came to be. "I wanted something to draw on a rug, and I couldn't find anything. I looked in the yard . . . and after a while I saw our cat, Malty, and I said to myself, 'He'll be good enough.' Then I got my old man to hold him down on this piece of burlap while I drew round him with a pencil. But I didn't know what to do with his tail. He was lying on it, so it didn't show in the picture. But no cats grow without tails, so my old man held it out nice and straight, then I just stuck it on here."[28]

Over the years, rugmakers have found that familiar subjects were usually the most effective. Seemingly, there is no subject that cannot be portrayed in a hooked rug, and we hope that contemporary rugmakers will try to find ideas for their rugs that relate to their own twentieth-century lives and experiences, and not rely on past designs and stenciled patterns. Drawing skill has always been less important than imagination and personal inventiveness in the making of great rugs.

144 (opposite below). This rug was clearly made by a person who had a good sense of humor and long experience with the happy chaos that takes place on Christmas Day in a house full of children. This scene is so animated and packed with detail that it merits being examined with a magnifying glass. c. 1910. 37" x 42". (Shelburne Museum, Inc.)

143 (above). This pastoral landscape is suffused with soft light and subtle pastels that capture the serenity of the time of day. A sensitively rendered collie keeps watch over a flock of sheep that have been consciously simplified into cloudlike forms that pick up some of the warm tones of the sunset sky. 1915–1925. 36" x 57". (Joseph and Ellen Wetherell)

145 (above). The puffin is a tame, curious bird found in Arctic regions such as Labrador. Here three perch in a row on ice caps under a sweeping Northern sky. c. 1930. 20″ x 25½″. (Allan L. Daniel)

146 (right). This rug, though probably not actually made for the Grenfell Mission, is certainly characteristic of the style and technique of hooking found in that area. It would seem that this portrays an actual house with a wide veranda, attic gable, and little roof over the front door. Border squares of alternating stripes harmonize with the rectangular fields of striations in the scene itself. c. 1910. 16″ x 24½″. (Judy and Paul Lenett)

147 (left). A simple house is rendered in a palette of subdued colors creating the impression of a soft winter's afternoon. c. 1920. 13″ x 20½″.

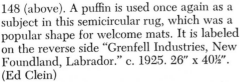

149 (above). The extremely simple forms of a polar bear against icebergs are beautifully composed to suit a very small rug made for the Grenfell Mission. c. 1920. 10″ x 12″. (Barbara Traub)

148 (above). A puffin is used once again as a subject in this semicircular rug, which was a popular shape for welcome mats. It is labeled on the reverse side "Grenfell Industries, New Foundland, Labrador." c. 1925. 26″ x 40½″. (Ed Clein)

150 (right). Dr. Wilfred Grenfell in Labrador. c. 1910. (Photograph courtesy The New York Public Library)

Labrador lies more than 600 miles north and 1000 miles east of New York City, and its area is the size of New England and New York State combined. When Dr. Wilfred Grenfell arrived there with a British hospital ship in 1892, he found the living conditions extremely bleak and primitive. For eight months of the year the inhabitants, who subsisted mainly on fishing and fur trapping, were virtually locked in by ice. The desolate villages had names like Came-By-Chance and Port Disappointment, and Grenfell himself referred to the territory as "the land God gave to Cain."

Grenfell decided to stay and devote his life to missionary work: establishing hospitals and encouraging productive activity during the months of idleness the people were forced to endure. Rug hooking was already a craft indigenous to the area before Dr. Grenfell came, but he was active in promoting it as a cottage industry, and in selling the mats and rugs the people produced.

The rugs generated by this colony had definite characteristics that reflected their circumstances and environment. They were made mainly from very thinly cut strips of wool and cotton-knit jerseys such as stockings, underwear, etc., so that every precious shred of fabric could be utilized. Even bits of burlap left over from the base were raveled and used in hooking. Burlap was much more durable than most fabric, and it was often dyed to give the appearance of cloth. The strips were very tightly hooked through every opening in the weave of the burlap foundation. These rugs were never clipped, and they have a dense, smooth surface, very similar to needlepoint. The subjects are all distinctively Northern. Although he did not actually teach the craft, the rugs made in the area of his mission have come to be called the "Grenfell" type.

151 (above). The ship *America*, seen in this rug, was built in Salem, Massachusetts, in 1804 and later became a successful privateer. 1890–1910. 36″ x 45″.

152 (below). Souvenirs of the China trade were not always trinkets, as this humorous rug reveals. Twentieth century. 29″ x 56″. (Photograph courtesy Sotheby Parke Bernet Inc.)

153 (above). This rug was hooked in 1902 by Laura Etta Clarke of Barrington, New Hampshire. She reversed this forty-six-star American flag from the way it is normally portrayed, perhaps as the result of the way she traced it. Dated 1902. 29″ x 37″. (Mr. and Mrs. Harley Trice II)

154 (opposite, below). This rug nostalgically recalls the loneliness of those left behind when a clipper ship put to sea. c. 1910. (Photograph courtesy Sotheby Parke Bernet Inc.)

155 (above). This is alleged to be a wedding rug, but the scene is so bizarre and highly subjective that it tempts us to speculate on the hidden significances that may be concealed in it. The rosy-cheeked moon-face with its penetrating stare may well be a mysterious personification of the moon itself. The bride (standing on her own tiny rug) seems to be appealing to it, or else offering thanks to it as the romantic power that has brought her the man of her dreams. The

young groom, perhaps even an imaginary one, has been isolated in his own light patch and surrounded by a vine that blossoms with hearts. Whatever these pictorial elements may mean, the maker of this rug had a special vision of love and in expressing it she carried the potentials of rugmaking to their ultimate as a folk-art form. 1900–1910. 29″ x 50″. Photograph courtesy Pine Cone Antiques. (Private collection)

156 (above). The sudden appearance of a friendly bull moose has apparently caught the duck hunter and his dog unprepared. c. 1910. 34" x 51".

157 (left). There is a happy cartoon quality to this smiling, bowlegged Thanksgiving turkey. Its plumage is striped with warm autumnal yellows and browns. 1910–1920. 18½" x 30". (Hastings House Antiques)

158 (below). This plump black cat appears to have been put on a pedestal by its owner, which perhaps accounts for its self-satisfied Cheshire-Cat-like smile. c. 1895. 26" x 44". (Michael and Mary Erlanger)

159 (opposite, above). Rugmakers often expressed their sense of humor through animal subjects. The expression of the eyes and the tufts of whiskers make this simple black fox an endearing and comical character. c. 1910. 22½" x 36". (Michael and Mary Erlanger)

160 (right). The impressive rooster in the foreground of this night scene seems to have gotten his times confused and is crowing prematurely at the moon. 1910–1920. 25″ x 39½″. (Barbara Johnson)

161 (below). A vivid rainbow border encircles two reindeer, their forms strongly delineated in brown and orange. Dated 1912. 28″ x 42″. (Allan L. Daniel)

162 (above). In this panorama of Niagara Falls the rugmaker has drawn on her skills as a Sunday painter in attempting to add a more naturalistic impression of water. Oil paint has actually been applied to the surface of the rug, making it the only painted hooked rug we have seen. c. 1925. 20″ x 38″. Photograph courtesy Country Inn Antiques.

163 (below). A solitary tree set against a mountain landscape is reduced to the essence of simplicity. Tweed fabric has been chosen to demarcate the sky and to give it an airy quality in contrast with the flat, solid shapes. 1910–1920. 29″ x 41″. (Ed Clein)

164 (opposite, above). Strength and energy are expressed in a whirlwind of blacks and blue-grays that model the body of this wide-eyed pony. Color is used with extraordinary sensitivity. The pastel colors of flowers, sky, and landscape melt together to create an atmosphere similar in feeling to an Impressionist painting. Dated 1929. 35″ x 41″. (Joseph and Ellen Wetherell)

165 (below). A wooden bead inserted as the eye of this otherwise placid horse lends it a lifelike quality. Crisp tufts of patterned grass line up in the foreground. But it is the erratic angularity of the sky that gives this rug its unique impact. It is such eccentric choices as this that give the best hooked rugs their unpredictable personalities. c. 1910. 28" x 39".

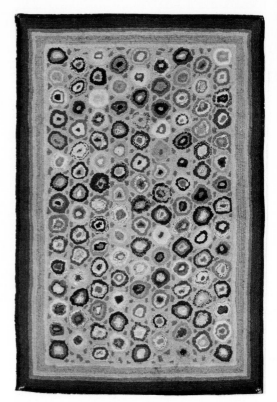

166 (above, left). This geometric pattern is sometimes referred to as Grandmother's Dream when found in a quilt. Bright colors break from the center in zigzags that evoke the feeling of some American Indian designs. c. 1915. 16½" x 30". (Ed Clein); 167 (below, left). Broken, angular patches of color, reminiscent of crazy quilts, are contained within a windowpane format. 1930–1940. 25" x 44". (Ed Clein); 168 (above, right). The maker of this rug has deliberately departed from regularity and consciously made each polka dot unique in both shape and color. 1920–1930. 35½" x 23½". (Ed Clein); 169 (below right). The popularity of Navajo blankets in the early part of the twentieth century is reflected in the bold geometry of this rug. 1920–1930. 30" x 43". (Ed Clein)

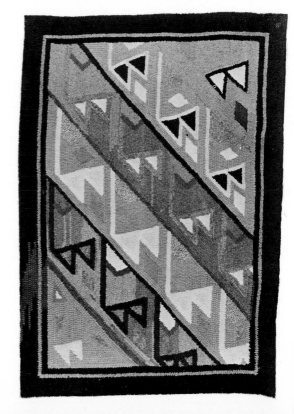

170 (left). Probably inspired by a Kazak carpet, this rug, worked in rich, elegant colors, has incorporated "art moderne" touches and uses restrained striations to emphasize its basic geometry. c. 1910. 54½″ x 69½″. (Jonathan Holstein and Gail van der Hoof)

172 (below). Many Oriental-style hooked rugs were made from patterns, as was this one, but the beauty of this rug is achieved through a sensitive choice of soft colors. c. 1910. 31½″ x 51″. (Jim and Marilyn Marinacio)

173 (bottom). Although this rug has an Oriental flavor due to the dark rich colors and symmetrical layout, the shapes used to achieve the effect are simple and characteristically American. c. 1910. 37″ x 24″. (Gary and Nancy Stass)

171 (below). Even though this rug is not a copy of any specific Persian carpet, its maker has obviously tried to capture the Oriental style and lushness. She has, however, retained the rug hooker's fondness for striations within the fields of color. c. 1910. 52½″ x 31″. (Ed and Mary Lou Jackson)

174 (above). Although favorite pets were often portrayed in rugs, human portraits are relatively uncommon. In this piece a simple dark background emphasizes the figures of a curly-haired little girl dressed in her best outfit and her smiling Saint Bernard. c. 1920. 28″ x 40″. (Carroll and Wendy Janis)

176 (above). A vision of snug security under an expressive night sky, this house has a light in every window and evidently a crackling fire in every fireplace. This rugmaker's sense of cheerful design is evident in the delight she took in the pattern of red bricks and the red-knobbed garden fence. 1930–1940. 31″ x 54″.

175 (opposite, below), 175a (below). The figures of the little girl and her dog look as if they might have been borrowed from an early *Little Orphan Annie* episode. The sentiment of the warm cozy home is a theme often used in rugs, although usually depicted from the exterior. The maker's sharp eye for detail has created a very real atmosphere for this pleasant living room. The pictures on the wall, the vases of flowers and candlesticks on the mantel, the fire crackling with warmth against the snowy landscape outside, and the accurate depiction of furnishings, convey a simplified but well-observed glimpse into a 1920s home. (Note the two hooked rugs at the right and left and the braided rug in the center). c. 1925. 35½″ x 70″. (Ed and Mary Lou Jackson)

177 (above). In this Canadian rug we find a very colorful use of "Grenfell type" hooking. It has been combined with a clipped, raised pile that gives a rounded surface texture to the animals in this pleasant farm scene. c. 1920. 29″ x 48″. (Michael and Mary Erlanger)

178 (below). A successful combination of colors and broad simple shapes is organized in this house scene. Variations on the triangle in the window curtains, flower beds, house gable, and tree base work harmoniously on a subtle abstract level. c. 1920. 26½″ x 38½″. (John and Jacqueline Sideli)

179 (above). A farm scene at milking time is tied together beautifully by a widening road. The road itself is hooked from raveled burlap, which adds interesting texture and practical durability to the rug. c. 1890. 18″ x 30″.

180 (below). A French flag flies from the roof of this imposing Victorian home, indicating that this rug is most likely of French-Canadian origin. The maker of this piece shows a keen eye for architectural detail and perspective. c. 1900. 24½″ x 40″. (Carroll and Wendy Janis)

181 (above). One of the motivations for hooked-rug makers of all periods was the desire to have some of the style and luxury that only the wealthy could afford, and so they borrowed images that appealed to them from whatever sources were available. By the 1920s and 1930s, illustrated magazines like *Town and Country* spread the fashionable look of Art Deco to a mass public. Certainly the maker of this rug aspired to "deco" sophistication when designing the sleek, stylized Dalmatian in its setting of exotic plants. c. 1930. 44" x 67½". (Michael and Mary Erlanger)

182 (left). A field of irregular diamonds is shaded with tones of blue and purple to create a composition of triangles. c. 1910. 39½" x 24½".

183 (above). Religious themes, although common in other household handicrafts, are hardly ever found in hooked rugs. Since these rugs were made to be walked on, religious subjects were probably considered inappropriate. In this special rug, however, the dynamics of the geometry and the intensity of the scarlet inscription express a strong, religious fervor. c. 1910. 28¼" x 50". (Herbert W. Hemphill, Jr.)

184 (right). Electric colors are here worked together to balance solid fields against zigzags within a simple format of squares. 1910–1920. 18" x 30". (Ed Clein)

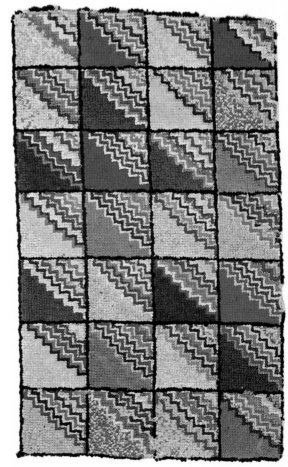

185 (above). Cupids supply the music for old-fashioned outdoor dancing as "Love Plays a Tune" for country courtship. Twentieth century. 29" x 53½". (Kelter-Malcé Antiques)

186 (below). Here we have a glimpse into what daily life was like in rural America where hooked rugs flourished. Everyone cheerfully pitches in with the chores, illustrating the optimism expressed in the homespun adage "Many Hands Make Little Work." Twentieth century. 35" x 61". (Sandy and Balene McCormick)

187 (above). Here good advice is given on the subject of love and marriage. In this elopement scene a young couple guided by Cupid rushes headlong toward the church despite the wild protestations of either a jilted suitor or a disapproving father at the left. Swirling lines in the background heighten the feeling of haste. Twentieth century. 29″ x 56″. (Burton and Helaine Fendelman)

188 (below). The moment of proposal takes place in the propriety of the family drawing room, as her happy parents beam their approval. And why not, since the young man seems to be a youthful carbon copy of the father. Twentieth century. 32″ x 51″. (Ed Clein)

The mob below
do stand & gape
Envelope us sir
In your firemans cape
And as for your own
Inscrutable stare
On the ground
We would rather be
Instead of up here!

By the 1920s and 1930s rug hooking as a cottage industry expanded, stimulated by an awakening interest in hooked rugs as "early American" antiques and also by an increasing market among the wave of motorists touring through New England. Women most likely hooked rugs with amusing, popular, and salable themes with the intention of trading them to a local roadside market, often in return for produce. Pictorial stories and anecdotes, usually accompanied by little poems in a consciously "down home" style, ranged from sentimental to humorously risqué. Firemen were apparently one of the favorite subjects, portrayed with tongue-in-cheek references to damsels in distress. Themes of love, marriage, domestic bliss, and domestic problems treated in a lighthearted way also had obvious appeal. Several examples are illustrated on the following pages.

189 (opposite). Twentieth century. 33″ x 49″.

190 (right). Twentieth century. 32″ x 50″.

191 (below). Twentieth century. 32½″ x 46″. Photograph courtesy Sotheby Parke Bernet Inc.

PLUCK MY HEART STRING CUPID WITH ABANDON AS OF YORE

AND SEND A MAN LIKE THIS ONE TO A LONELY WIDOWS DOOR

WHY WAIT THE FULL MOON??

192, 193, 194, 195, 196, 197. The rugs shown on these two pages were all formerly in the collection of James L. Hutchinson. They were sold at auction in various sales throughout the 1940s. Photographs reproduced from auction catalogues, courtesy Sotheby Parke Bernet Inc.

HERE HOOKED IS A PICTURE OF MY HUSBANDS KIN ILL BE GLAD WHEN I DIE AND DONT SEE THEM AGAIN

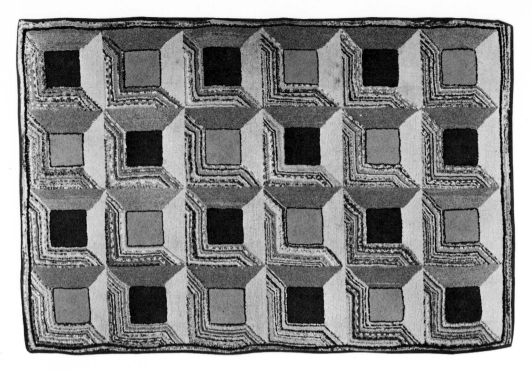

198 (above). Here is a sophisticated treatment of spatial illusion based on the square. The alternation of light and dark blocks adds variety to the interior space that has been created. c. 1950. 29″ x 47½″. (Kelter-Malcé Antiques)

199 (left). In this rug, based on a pattern called Variable Star, colors have been chosen so that the eye can let a number of different patterns emerge. 1940–1950. 29″ x 46½″. (Kelter-Malcé Antiques)

200 (below). This composition of squares depends on variations in tone to achieve its windowpane effect. c. 1920. 35½″ x 18″. (Sara Melvin)

201 (above). People who are highly sophisticated in their knowledge of the fine arts have often been attracted to "primitive" crafts as a means of expression. In this rug Marguerite Zorach has created a splendid nude in the French decorative style of the 1920s. c. 1925. 29″ x 48″. (Dahlov Ipcar)

202 (above). Dahlov Ipcar, the daughter of the artist who made the nude above, has created here a complicated graphic design centered on a leopard and a tiger. The animals and the luxuriant tropical foliage create an exotic atmosphere that is reminiscent of the work of Henri Rousseau. 1974. 37″ x 59″. (Dahlov Ipcar)

203 (above). The maker of this rug has given the family automobile a humorous, animated personality. 1920–1930. 20″ x 36″. (Kelter-Malcé Antiques)

204 (left). A girl stands in the yard of her large house, while the space around it and the sky above are filled with an imaginative assortment of floating animals. c. 1910. 26½″ x 46½″. (Davida Deutsch Antiques)

205 (left). This rug was worked from a simple outline pattern called the Old New England Coachline, produced by Burnham and Co. in the 1930s. The dramatic swirling clouds and mountains and the foreground of cheerful flowers, however, are all the product of this rugmaker's personal inventiveness. c. 1935. (Betty Sterling)

206 (above). In this portrait of a happy family of cats the pleased parents watch over their playful kittens. c. 1930. 37" x 69".

207 (right). Few creatures of the animal kingdom escaped the rugmaker's notice. Even the customarily unwelcome skunk has been chosen as a worthy subject. 1920–1930. 20" x 34". (John and Jacqueline Sideli)

208 (right). Quintuplet basset pups pose for a group portrait. 1940–1950. 22" x 35".

209 (left). Rugmakers often borrowed their designs from diverse sources. In the case of this rug a small watercolor *fraktur*[29] has been translated into a rather large rug made over 100 years later. The tulips, stars, and hex signs are typically Pennsylvanian. c. 1940. 87" x 39½". (David and Susan Cunningham)

Mary Mac Franklin is a contemporary rugmaker who still holds to the old techniques of rug hooking, even hand-dyeing wool in the traditional manner. As we have pointed out, many rugs throughout the period of hooked-rug making contain subjects, details, and symbols of personal interest to rugmakers and their families, and Mary Mac has kindly explained to us what the details in her rugs signify and why she included them.

210 (opposite, above). This "autobiographical rug," as the maker Mary Mac Franklin calls it, is filled with words, objects, and numbers that have special meaning to her. A librarian for many years, Mrs. Franklin has included names and quotations from some of her favorite authors. Trademarks of products used by her—the logo of *The New Yorker* magazine, the wool industry symbol, and a Jack Daniels bottle—are shown with such household items as her often-used coffee cup and her grandmother's clock. An Indian head penny, a miniature shoe, and an antique sign symbolize things she collects, whereas a book, a bridge hand, a rolling pin, and a rug hook represent some of her recreational activities. Address numbers of the Franklins' former homes are included around the inner border. 1974. 72" x 72". (Mary Mac Franklin)

211 (below). Tennessee was the home state of both Mary Mac and her husband Robert Franklin, and across her hooked-rug map of the state she has outlined the old Route 70, between Knoxville and Memphis, which is the road her husband traveled to visit her during their courtship. Among the many symbols of state pride are a Tennessee walking horse, the main building of the University of Tennessee at Knoxville, and Andrew Johnson's log cabin. 1959. 24″ x 70″. (Mary Mac Franklin)

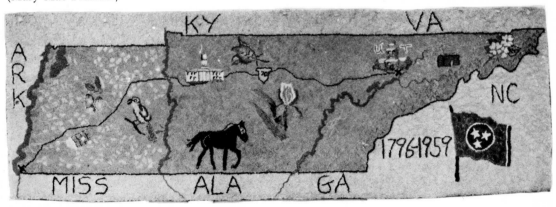

ILLUSTRATIONS OF TECHNIQUES

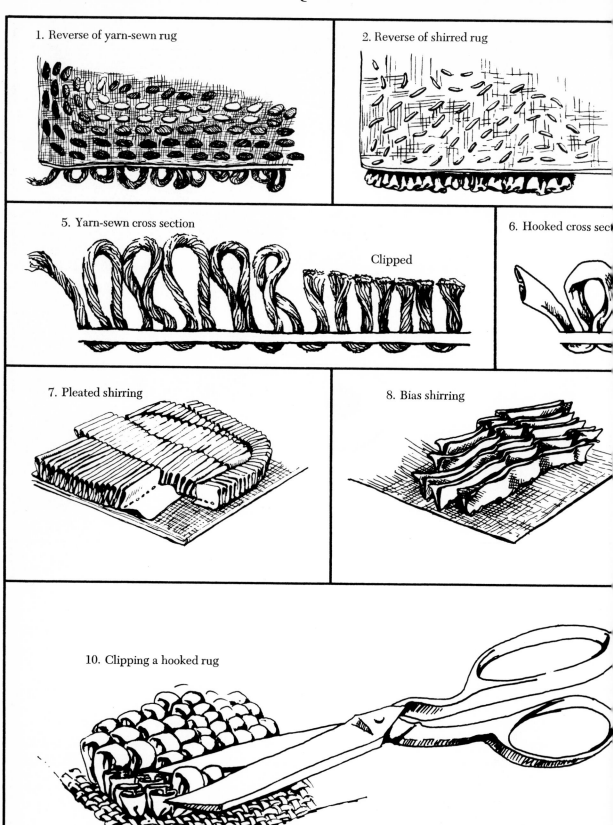

1. Reverse of yarn-sewn rug

2. Reverse of shirred rug

5. Yarn-sewn cross section

Clipped

6. Hooked cross sec[

7. Pleated shirring

8. Bias shirring

10. Clipping a hooked rug

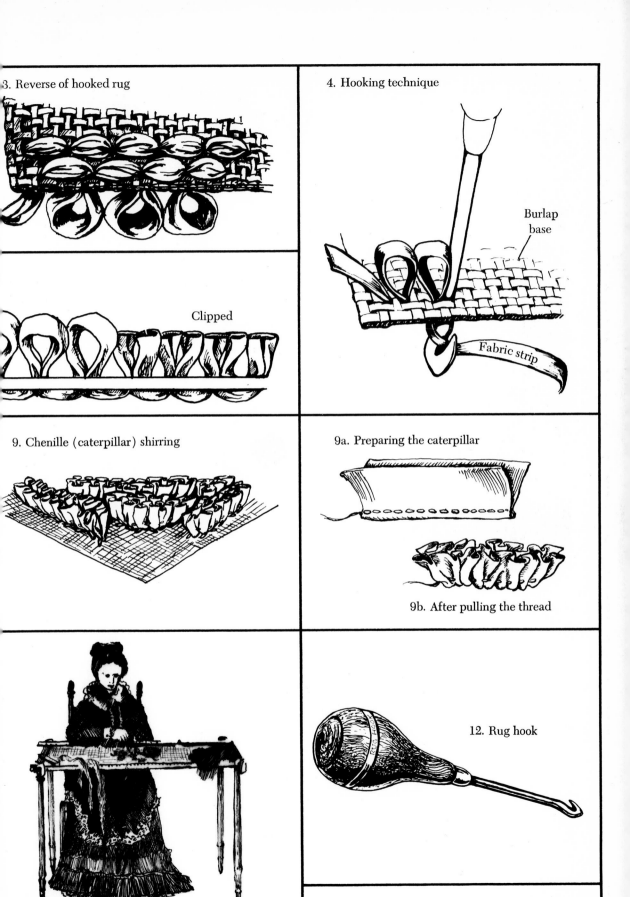

3. Reverse of hooked rug

4. Hooking technique

Burlap base

Clipped

Fabric strip

9. Chenille (caterpillar) shirring

9a. Preparing the caterpillar

9b. After pulling the thread

11. Hooking at a frame

12. Rug hook

Drawn by Kay Hines

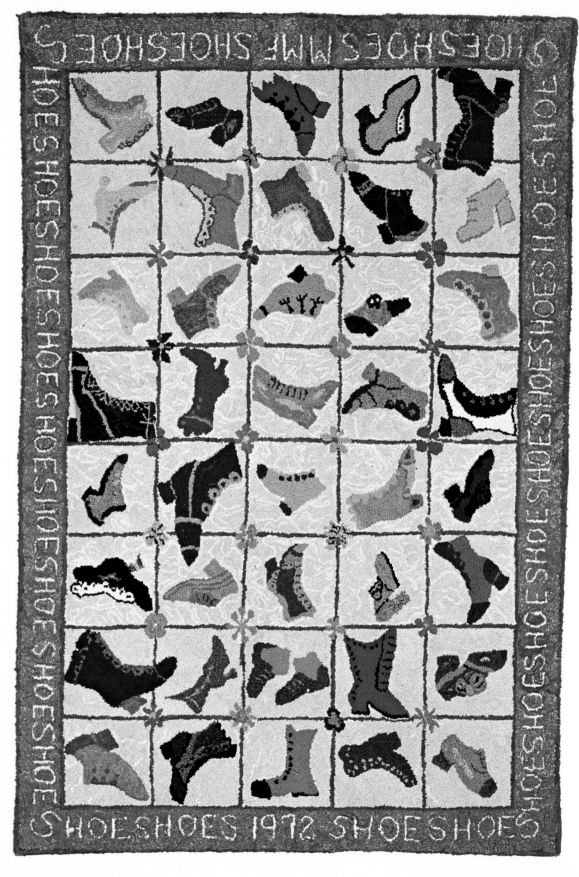

NOTES

1. Marion Day Iverson, "The Bed Rug in Colonial America," The Magazine *Antiques* (January 1964), p. 107.

2. Benjamin Franklin, in a letter to Miss Georgiana Shipley, 1772: "Here Skugg lies snug as a bug in a rug."

3. Marion Day Iverson, "The Bed Rug in Colonial America," The Magazine *Antiques* (January 1964), p. 107.

4. Rodris Roth, *Floor Coverings in 18th-Century America* (Washington, D.C.: Smithsonian Institution, 1967), p. 53.

5. *Ibid.*

6. Noah Webster, *Dictionary of the English Language*, 1828.

7. Nina Fletcher Little in *Floor Coverings in New England Before 1850* (Sturbridge, Mass.: Old Sturbridge Village, 1967) mentions some later yarn-sewn rugs made on burlap, which would carry the technique of yarn sewing into the late 1850s, when burlap was introduced to North America. Mrs. Little states: ". . . it is always unwise to set a terminal date for handcrafts which in some localities persisted long after they had disappeared in others" (p. 33).

8. *Reed stitched*: For a long time the term *reed-stitched* was used to describe all yarn-sewn rugs. Reed-stitching was, however, only one technique that could be applied to yarn sewing, where regular, conforming rows were desired. A reed, quill, or other similarly flexible device was placed on the fabric base to follow the design, and then yarn was sewn around it continuously along its length to make a row of loops. When the reed was pulled out, the surface loops were of uniform height, and the stitches were pulled flat against the fabric base. In almost all the examples of yarn-sewn rugs we have examined, the loops are cut, and we assume that in some cases a cutting edge may have been attached to the reed itself, so that it slit open the loops as it was withdrawn.

In the case of hooked rugs, *reed-stitch* refers to uniform rows of loops. In hooking, however, the regulating device must be inserted separately for each loop. Mechanical devices for hooking, which gauged the desired height of the loops, have been used to achieve the same effect.

9. *Tow*: a coarse fabric made from the shorter, less desirable flax fibers.

10. *Tambour work*: a type of embroidery stitch made with a fine needle that has a tiny hook at the end of it. Thread was held underneath a sheer fabric, stretched over a circular frame, consisting of two hoops, one fitting inside the other. The thread was pulled up through the foundation with the hook, forming very fine, successive chain stitches. Originating in India, this technique was used in America primarily to decorate clothing, especially collars and cuffs. Tambour work gets its name from the French word for drum.

11. Elizabeth Waugh and Edith Foley, *Collecting Hooked Rugs* (New York: The Century Co., 1927), pp. 7–8.

12. Marius Barbeau, "The Origin of the Hooked Rug," The Magazine *Antiques* (1947), p. 110.

13. Ella Shannon Bowles, *Homespun Handicrafts* (Philadelphia: J. B. Lippincott Company, 1931).

14. Virginia D. Parslow, "Hooked Rugs," *The Concise Encyclopedia of American Antiques*, ed. H. Comstock (New York: Hawthorn Books, Inc., 1965), pp. 350–352.

15. Allen H. Eaton, *Handicrafts of the Southern Highlands* (New York: Dover Publications, Inc., 1973). An unabridged republication of the work originally published in 1937 by Russell Sage Foundation, New York.

16. Waugh and Foley, *Collecting Hooked Rugs*.

17. Lydia Le Baron Walker, *Homecraft Rugs* (New York: Frederick A. Stokes & Co., 1929).

18. The Wolverhampton Museum has what is believed to be the oldest rag rug made in Great Britain. It was made from scraps of woolen uniforms worn by soldiers who had fought at the Battle of Waterloo in 1815.

19. Thrumming has been used in Great Britain for centuries for making mats. Strands of yarn too short for weaving were poked through a cloth base, the two open ends of each piece were left standing out about an inch, with a looped end on the reverse side of the mat. The thrums were set closely together and the tightness of the weave and the pressure of the thrums wedged against each other held the mat together. Thrumming was apparently not confined to mats. In Shakespeare's *The Merry Wives of Windsor* Falstaff makes an opportune escape disguised in a large gown and a "thrummed hat" belonging to a lady described as "the fat woman of Brentford."

20. Bertram M. Downing, an antique dealer in Greenwich, Connecticut, in the 1870s, specialized in old hooked and sewn rugs and antique English carpets. He was succeeded by his son Bertram, Jr., who also specialized in antique hooked rugs and their repair.

21. In some instances women used strands of unraveled burlap to hook with, especially on borders, as it proved exceptionally durable for daily wear. Many of the rugmakers utilized commercially dyed knitting yarns to hook their rugs, especially during the twentieth century.

22. The "Waldoboro-type" rug takes its name from the town of Waldoboro, Maine. This style of hooked rug developed in and around Waldoboro, and it is distinguished by a deep pile that is clipped and sculptured so that elements of the

212 (opposite). Another rug by Mary Mac Franklin shows a marvelous array of old-fashioned footwear, whose designs were inspired by pieces in her own collection of miniature antique shoes. 1972. 36″ x 54″. (Mary Mac Franklin)

213 (above). Rugmaking was a form of folk art that encompassed many aspects of small-town and rural life. In hooked rugs people found an outlet for creativity, and they used the rugs as a canvas on which to depict what they saw around them, to commemorate special events, and to express sentiments and personal messages both visually and verbally. They were decorative yet practical items that were sometimes made to be given as gifts. This Good Luck rug was possibly intended for a new home or a new bride. c. 1880. 32″ x 61″. (Michael and Mary Erlanger)

design stand out from the background in the style of bas-relief. The most typical examples were wreath or oval floral compositions in vivid colors against dark or black backgrounds.

Waldoboro and its vicinity was settled in the early nineteenth century by German immigrants, who brought with them the knowledge of European craft techniques. Sculptured, deep-pile carpets were made in areas of Holland, France, and Germany, and work in deep pile had been introduced in Canada by seventeenth-century French settlers. The European carpets were sewn using measuring devices to achieve various heights of the pile, and the Waldoboro settlers adapted these techniques to American rug hooking to produce extraordinary rugs with a pile frequently more than one half inch deep.

We know from Mrs. Priscilla Creamer of Waldoboro, Maine, who was an antiques dealer there, with her husband in the 1920s and 1930s, that these rugs were hooked primarily for personal enjoyment and were intended to be decorative showpieces rather than utilitarian floor mats. The uneven surfaces are luxurious in texture but highly impractical for walking on. We also learned from Mrs. Creamer that sculptured, high-pile rugs made in the Waldoboro area were usually hooked on linen, and although the colors included vivid reds, pinks, and oranges, yellow was almost never used. The term *Waldoboro-type* is now used generically

to refer to rugs with sculptured pile surfaces.

23. An illustration of an early nineteenth-century carriage cover embroidered on linen with an almost identical motif appears in *The Decorative Arts of Sweden* by Iona Plath (New York: Dover Publications, Inc., 1965), p. 30.

24. Many mechanical hooking devices were invented at the end of the nineteenth century that could use wool yarn or cut strips of cloth. Many hooked rugs that are so-called reed-stitched (i.e. straight even rows of loops both horizontally and vertically) are made with a mechanical hook. The "punch-hook," which is still in use today, is more like a mechanical needle than a hook. It is worked on the reverse side of the rug with a gauge for measuring the height of the loops. Although rugs made with a punch-hook can be graphically impressive, they lack the texture and individuality that hand-hooking can produce.

25. *The House Beautiful* (July 1928), p. 58.

26. Allan H. Eaton, *Handicrafts of the Southern Highlands* (New York: Dover Publications, Inc., 1973), p. 77.

27. *Ibid.*, p. 221.

28. *The House Beautiful* (July 1928), p. 87.

29. The design of this rug copies a bookplate from the Bible of Catherina Guth illustrated in *Pennsylvania German Illustrated Manuscripts* by Henry Bornemann (New York: Dover Publications, Inc, 1973), pl. 33.

Cleaning. Hooked rugs, especially after years of use, require special and careful attention. The nature of the hooking technique and the frequent presence of old fabrics and home-dyed colors dictate special handling when cleaning these rugs. First the *don'ts*: don't put a hooked rug into a washing machine, even on the so-called gentle cycle. Don't shake out or beat a hooked rug, since shaking, beating, or even vacuuming from the back can dislodge the fabric from the foundation. Don't, unless absolutely necessary, submerge a rug in water; surface cleaning is usually all that is required.

If your rug is only slightly dirty, you can vacuum the front using the low-suction control, or gently sweep it with a soft brush. As mentioned above, do not vacuum the back, use a brush instead. After sweeping or vacuuming, surface cleaning with a wet sponge or soft brush with cold water and a mild soap may be required. Using mostly suds and very little of the water itself (taking care not to soak the base), clean with a circular motion on one six-inch-square area at a time, overlapping each area successively. Check for color fastness. (Printed calicoes and woven plaids are less likely to run than solid-color fabrics, which are frequently home-dyed.) A light second sponging with plain water will remove most of the remaining soap. We have had good success with such commercial rug cleaners as Glamorine and Bissel, using a sponge and warm water and following the directions on the package. After the rug is thoroughly dry, loosened dirt and lint can be vacuumed out of the rug using the low-suction setting. If surface cleaning proves inadequate, the rug can be cleaned by submerging it in cold water and using a soft brush or sponge with a mild soap. Be sure to rinse the rug several times, and special care must be taken when the rug is soaking wet. Do not wring or squeeze the water out of the rug. Instead, roll the rug in towels with the front side of the rug out. Do not hang the wet rug on a clothesline or on a rod. The weight of a wet rug held with clothespins can break the foundation of an old rug, and hanging a rug over a line or rod can put a permanent crease in it. Let the rug dry on a towel or on grass for a day on its front side and another day on the back.

Storage and shipping. *ROLL, DON'T FOLD, ALWAYS WITH THE RIGHT SIDE OUT. Folding* a hooked rug will break the base, especially if anything heavy is set on top. Rolling with the base out puts an unnecessary strain on the burlap and weakens the foundation. If a rug is to be stored for a long period, use a sheet or cloth to wrap it but don't use an airtight plastic bag. Textiles need to breathe, and they will sometimes rot or mildew in a plastic bag. Don't put a hooked rug (or any other early textiles) in a hot, dry closet or attic. The base of a rug can dry out and become brittle, destroying the strength and durability of the rug. Cardboard rolls from Christmas wrapping paper or fabric-store throwaways are excellent cores for rolling a rug.

Condition counts when buying a hooked rug. Professional restoration is available, but it is usually expensive, and sometimes rugs that are structurally unsound cannot be repaired. The most important thing to check for in a rug is whether or not it is dried out and brittle. You can usually ascertain this by lightly squeezing a portion of the rug in your hand. It should feel supple and pliable. A rug with a weakened or rotted base is easily damaged or even destroyed just by normal use, and rugs in this condition are very difficult to repair. Hold a rug up to the light to look for small holes or breaks (these can usually be repaired). Most old hooked rugs have been repaired in the course of time, and the presence of patches on the back of a rug does not lessen its desirability if the restoration has been well done with colors and cloth in the same type as the original. Rugs are frequently rebound to cover wear at the edges, and rebinding does not reduce a rug's desirability if the work has been done correctly. The only proper way to repair a hole in a hooked rug is to sew a small burlap patch to the base and rehook the missing area. A rug that has been repaired with sewing thread will not hold up if used underfoot. Virtually all old hooked rugs were worked on burlap or homespun linen, and hooked rugs on white monk's cloth (some of which were made in Taiwan in the 1950s) should be presumed to be modern. Hooked rugs that are used on a hard floor should have a thin rubber base beneath them to help insure longer wear.

Hanging. Delicate and prized rugs can often be enjoyed more as wall hangings than as floor coverings. Although rugs are frequently hung to protect them from damage, improper hanging can often do more damage to a rug than keeping it on the floor. Never use nails or staples at the top of a rug that you expect to hang for any period of time. A rug should be supported so that the weight is evenly distributed. The best way to accomplish this is with a plywood backing cut one half inch smaller than the rug in both dimensions. The rug should first be mounted on a burlap or canvas backing cut about five inches larger than the rug. This border of new fabric is then stretched and tacked or stapled to the back of the plywood. Rugs that have a separate backing that is tacked evenly across the rug can be mounted by sewing a sleeve to the backing and using a thin slat of wood that is put through the sleeve and attached to the wall. This method is recommended only if the sleeve is sewn to a backing and *not sewn through the base or the loops of the rug.*

SELECTED BIBLIOGRAPHY

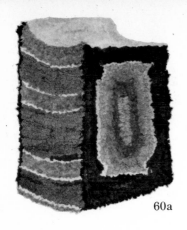

60a

Books

Bowles, Ella Shannon. *Handmade Rugs*. Boston: Little, Brown & Co., 1927.

Cahill, Holger. *American Folk Art, the Art of the Common Man in America, 1750–1900* (catalogue). New York: The Museum of Modern Art, 1932.

Cuyler, Susanne. *The High-Pile Rug Book*. New York: Harper & Row, 1974.

Eaton, Allen H. *Handicrafts of the Southern Highlands*. New York: Dover Publications, Inc., 1973. An unabridged republication of the work originally published in 1937 by Russell Sage Foundation, New York.

Frost, Edward Sands. *Hooked Rug Patterns*. Dearborn, Mich.: Greenfield Village and Henry Ford Museum, 1970.

Hicks, Amy Mali. *The Craft of Hand-Made Rugs*. New York: Empire State Book Co., 1936.

Hornung, Clarence P. *Treasury of American Design*. New York: Harry N. Abrams, 1972.

Kent, W. W. *Rare Hooked Rugs*. Springfield, Mass.: Pond-Ekberg Co., 1941.

Kopp, Joel, and Kopp, Kate. *Hooked Rugs in the Folk Art Tradition* (catalogue). New York: Museum of American Folk Art, 1974.

Little, Frances. *Early American Textiles*. New York: The Century Co., 1931.

Little, Nina Fletcher. *Floor Coverings in New England Before 1850*. Sturbridge, Mass.: Old Sturbridge Village, 1967.

Parslow, Virginia D. "Hooked Rugs," in *The Concise Encyclopedia of American Antiques*. Edited by H. Comstock. New York: Hawthorn Books, 1965.

Ramsey, L. G. G. *The Complete Encyclopedia of Antiques*. Re-

print. New York: Hawthorn Books, 1967.

Rex, Stella Hay. *Choice Hooked Rugs*. Englewood Cliffs, N.J.: Prentice-Hall, Inc., 1953.

Ries, Estelle H. *American Rugs*. Cleveland, Ohio: The World Publishing Co., 1950.

Roth, Rodris. *Floor Coverings in 18th-Century America*. Washington, D.C.: Smithsonian Institution, 1967.

Safford, Carleton L., and Bishop, Robert. "The Bed Rug," in *America's Quilts and Coverlets*. New York: E. P. Dutton & Co., Inc., 1972.

Walker, Lydia Le Baron. *Homecraft Rugs*. New York: Frederick A. Stokes & Co., 1929.

Warren, William L., and Callister, J. Herbert. *Bed Ruggs 1722–1833*. Hartford, Conn.: Wadsworth Atheneum, 1972.

Waugh, Elizabeth, and Foley, Edith. *Collecting Hooked Rugs*. New York: The Century Co., 1927.

Articles in Periodicals

Albee, Helen R. "Developing a Home Industry." *Craftsman Magazine* (May 1908).

"American Hooked Rugs." *The Arts* (May 1921).

Barbeau, Marius. "The Hooked Rug: Its Origin." *Transactions of the Royal Society of Canada*. 3rd series. (1942).

———. "The Origin of the Hooked Rug." *Antiques* (August 1947).

Carey, Mary Johnson. "Hooked Rugs." *The Antiquarian* (May 1925).

Clarke, J., and Clarke, F. "American Rugs in Wool and Cotton Chenille." *Arts and Decoration* (March 1930).

"Distinctive American Rugs: Designed and Woven in the Homes of Country Women." *The Craftsman* 10 (1906).

Dodge, Irene. "Philena Moxley's Embroidery Stamps." The Magazine *Antiques* (August 1972).

The Embroidery Stamping Blocks. Pamphlet. Wenham, Conn.: Wenham Historical Society.

Grenfell, Wilfred T. "The Hooked Mat Industry." *Among the Deep Sea Fishers* (May 10, 1913).

———. "The St. Anthony Mat Industry." *Among the Deep Sea Fish-*

ers (January 1917).

Holway, Katharine Quincy. "American Hooked and Other Rugs." *The Antiquarian* (August 1929).

Iverson, Marion Day. "The Bed Rug in Colonial America." The Magazine *Antiques* (January 1964).

The Journal of American Folklore (October–December 1943).

Law, Margaret Lathrop. "Hooked Rugs of Nova Scotia." *House Beautiful* (July 1928).

Leitch, Adelaide. "Pictures on Brin —The Grenfell Hooked Mats." *Canadian Geographical Journal* (February 1958).

MacLaughlin, Marjorie. "Landscape Rugs in Quebec." *Canadian Geographical Journal* (December 1930).

Ramsay, J. "Note on the Geography of Hooked Rugs." *Antiques* (December 1930).

"Rug for the Queen." *Christian Science Monitor*, magazine section, June 3, 1939.

"Rugs: Hooked and Patchwork." *Antiques* (March 1931).

Safford, Carleton L. "Mrs. Elenore Blackstone's Hooked Rugs." *The Herald*. Greenfield Village and Henry Ford Museum, 1973.

Traquair, Ramsey. "Hooked Rugs in Canada." *Canadian Geographical Journal* (May 1943).

Auction Catalogues of Special Interest

Hutchinson Collection. *Early American Hooked Rugs*. The Anderson Galleries, March 29, 1927. Sale No. 2153.

Schernikow Collection. *Rare Hooked Rugs*. The Anderson Galleries, April 16, 1929. Sale No. 2336.

Shoemaker Collection. *Hook Rugs Made in America*. The Anderson Galleries, May 9, 1923. Sale No. 1746.

Shoemaker Collection. *Early American Hook Rugs*. The American Art Galleries, New York, April 30, 1924.

C. M. Traver Collection. *Rare American Antiques and Rare Hooked Rugs*. The Anderson Galleries, April 17, 1925. Sale No. 1952.

Wettleson Collection. *Early Colonial Hook Rugs*. The Anderson Galleries, January 4, 1924. Sale No. 1791.